WILLIAMS-SONOMA

Chicken for Dinner

GENERAL EDITOR

Chuck Williams

RECIPES

Heidi Haughy Cusick

PHOTOGRAPHY

Richard Eskite

Oxmoor House®

OXMOOR HOUSE INC.

Oxmoor House books are distributed by
Sunset Books
80 Willow Road, Menlo Park, CA 94025
Phone: (650) 321-3600 Fax: (650) 324-1532

Vice President/General Manager: Rich Smeby
Director of Special Sales: Gary Wright
Oxmoor House and Sunset Books are divisions of
Southern Progress Corporation

WILLIAMS-SONOMA

Founder and Vice-Chairman: Chuck Williams
Book Buyer: Cecilia Michaelis

WELDON OWEN INC.

Cheif Executive Officer: John Owen
President: Terry Newell
Chief Operating Officer: Larry Partington
Vice President, International Sales: Stuart Laurence
Associate Publisher: Lisa Atwood
Managing Editor: JJudith Dunham
Consulting Editor: Norman Kolpas
Copy Editor: Sharon Silva
Design: Kari Perin, Perin+Perin
Production Director: Stephanie Sherman
Production Manager: Jen Dalton
Production Editor: Sarah Lemas
Food Stylist: George Dolese
Prop Stylist: Sara Slavin
Photo Production Coordinator: Juliann Harvey
Photo Assistant: Lara Hata
Food Styling Assistant: Jill Sorensen
Glossary Illustrations: Alice Harth

A NOTE ON WEIGHTS AND MEASURES

All recipes include customary U.S. and metric
measurements. Metric conversions are based on a
standard developed for these books and have been
rounded off. Actual weights may vary.

The Williams-Sonoma Lifestyles Series
conceived and produced by Weldon Owen Inc.
814 Montgomery Street, San Francisco, CA 94133

In collaboration with Williams-Sonoma
3250 Van Ness Avenue, San Francisco, CA 94109

Separations by Colourscan Overseas Co. Pte. Ltd.
Printed in Singapore by Tien Wah Press (Pte.) Ltd.

A WELDON OWEN PRODUCTION

Copyright © 1998 Weldon Owen Inc.
All rights reserved, including the right of reproduc-
tion in whole or in part in any form.

First printed in 1998
10 9 8 7 6 5 4 3 2

Library of Congress
Cataloging-in-Publication Data

Goldstein, Joyce Esersky.
    Soup for Supper / general editor, Chuck
Williams; recipes, Joyce Goldstein; photography,
Richard Eskite.
        p. cm. — (Williams-Sonoma lifestyles)
    Includes index.
    ISBN 0-8487-2620-0
    1. Soups 1. Williams, Chuck II. Title.
III. Series.
TX757.G55 1998
641.8'13—dc21   98-9457
                                        CIP

A NOTE ON NUTRITIONAL ANALYSIS

Each recipe is analyzed for significant nutrients per
serving. Not included in the analysis are ingredients
that are optional or added to taste, or are suggested
as an alternative or substitution either in the recipe
or in the recipe introduction or accompanying tip.
In recipes that yield a range of servings, the analysis
is for the middle of that range.

Contents

Welcome

Chicken has become the most familiar and comforting main course we know. It is what we turn to when we want simple and satisfying fare for the dinner table. That is why the title of this book strikes such a heartwarming chord in most people, whatever their dinnertime preferences may be.

The good taste of chicken is, of course, its greatest asset. But chicken is also arguably the most versatile meat in the market. As the step-by-step instructions on the following pages show, you can cook it by nearly any method you like. Chicken readily pairs with almost any kind of seasoning, from the mildest to the spiciest, the most familiar to the most exotic. For proof, look no further than the chicken recipes that form the centerpiece of this book, along with the great diversity of first courses, side dishes, and desserts that accompany them.

Combine that versatility with how easy and inexpensive it is to buy and cook chicken, and you can see why even the humblest chicken dish can bring so much pleasure to host and guests alike. I hope this book will inspire you to serve chicken for dinner soon and often.

Chuck Williams

Serving Chicken for Dinner

Pick your serving pieces for a chicken dinner based on the recipe you've prepared, the style of the occasion you've planned, and what is already available in your own kitchen.

Bringing Versatility to Your Table

The phrase "chicken for dinner" instantly conveys the strong impression that a meal will be special, no matter what the occasion. The remarkable versatility of chicken means that it can star at a homey weeknight family meal, a casual party for friends, or a special supper intended to impress.

Chicken is easy to cook, making it admirably suited to busy lifestyles. Chicken pieces can be ready to eat in a matter of minutes, while a whole roast chicken (pages 10–11, 30, 78) cooks with little attention once in the oven. That leaves you time to attend to the sort of simple first courses, side dishes, and desserts that will best complement your meal (pages 16–17).

Selecting Chicken at the Market

As you look through the chicken recipes in this book, you'll see that they are free of the terms *broiler-fryer,* which designates a young chicken weighing 2½–4 pounds (1.25–2 kg); *roasting chicken,* referring to a larger bird of 3½–8 pounds (1.75–4 kg) destined for the oven; and *stewing chicken,* an older, tougher bird weighing 3–5 pounds (1.5–2.5 kg) that is best suited to slow, moist cooking. Such terms have become largely meaningless to the vast majority of us who buy whatever chicken is available in local markets, which offer the convenience of precut pieces and even boned and skinned chicken breasts.

That said, you should buy the best-quality chicken you can find. For the finest flavor and texture, seek out chickens raised on a diet of grain, whether in organized breeding farms or as "free-range" birds allowed to hunt and peck. Read the labels on any packaged chicken, whether whole or pieces. Your best guarantee of quality is to select products that specifically state that they have been minimally processed and are all natural, without artificial ingredients or antibiotics. For optimal freshness, check the labels as well, or ask your butcher, to make sure the chicken was produced locally.

Presenting Chicken at Table

Although the more elegant chicken preparations can be individually plated, a selection of platters is perhaps most useful for serving the casual chicken dishes featured in this book. A platter can be used both for serving family style and for presenting whole roast chicken.

If you plan to carve a whole chicken at the table, it's a good idea to use a wooden carving platter with a grooved surface that prevents slippage. For more informal or family-style meals, you could just as well carve the chicken on a cutting board in the kitchen (page 11) before arranging the pieces on a platter to bring to the table.

It is also a good idea to have on hand attractive cooking vessels that double as serving pieces, such as dutch ovens, covered casseroles, or clay bakers (at right).

Serving Wine or Beer with Chicken Dishes

Chicken is prepared in so many ways that it lends itself to matching with a wide range of wines.

In general, serve light white wines with lighter chicken dishes, particularly those delicately seasoned or sauced. As seasonings or other ingredients grow more robust, or when flavors intensify as they do when a whole chicken is roasted, serve a rich white or a light red wine. Grilled or fried chicken and Asian dishes are well suited to ice-cold beer.

Roasting and Carving

Easy Steps for Success

For perfectly roasted chicken, truss the bird and place in a preheated 425°F (220°C) oven. Immediately reduce the oven temperature to 350°F (180°C) and cook for 20 minutes per pound. If you like, baste once or twice toward the end of the cooking time to ensure a moist result.

TRUSSING

1. To be sure the oven's heat circulates fully around the chicken, place it on a V-shaped rack inside a roasting dish or pan. Tie kitchen string securely around the ends of the drumsticks to bind them together.

2. To secure the chicken's wings, keeping them from splaying outward as it roasts, take the triangular tip of each wing and tuck it snugly underneath the body. Roast as directed.

Try any of the following (left to right): skinning the chicken and rubbing the meat with a paste of herbs or spices, surrounding it with aromatic vegetables in the roasting pan, or tucking seasonings between the skin and flesh.

TESTING FOR DONENESS

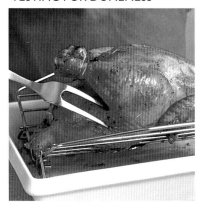

To test for doneness, pierce the thigh with a long fork or skewer; the juices should run clear. Alternatively, insert an instant-read thermometer into the thickest part of the thigh or the breast, avoiding the bone; the meat should register 185°F (85°C) in the thigh or 170°F (77°C) in the breast.

2. Next, separate the thigh from the drumstick, cutting between them down to the joint. Then, carefully cut through the joint and the tendons that surround it. Use the same method to cut off the chicken's wings.

CARVING

1. To carve a whole chicken, begin by removing the legs. Move a drumstick to locate the hip joint. With a sharp knife, cut through the tendons and joint to remove the leg. Repeat with the other leg.

3. If you're carving a large chicken for serving on a platter, cut off the breast meat in long, thin slices parallel to the rib cage. For a small chicken, you can remove the entire breast from each side, starting at the breastbone and cutting down along the ribs.

THE WISHBONE

One of the bonuses of serving a whole roast chicken is the tradition of the wishbone, the bird's horseshoe-shaped collarbone. As two people hold the opposite ends, they both make silent wishes and pull. The wish comes true for whoever gets the larger piece.

The ritual has its roots in ancient Etruria, now part of Italy, where sacred chickens were kept in temples and, by their pecking of grains, were believed to predict the future. When a bird died, its collarbone would be saved and used as a talisman for wish making. The ancient Romans added the twist of two people breaking the bone.

Cutting Up a Chicken

Rediscovering a Lost Art

Food stores make cut-up chickens so readily available today that you might, at first, see no point in doing it yourself. But you can do the job easily, especially with the help of a pair of poultry shears such as those shown here. Save the trimmings for the stockpot (page 15).

SEPARATING INTO PIECES

1. Using poultry shears, cut through the skin between each thigh and the body. Move the legs to locate the joints; cut through the joints on each side to remove the legs.

2. Use the same method of removing the legs to cut off the wings. Then, cut through the rib bones on either side of the breast to remove the back.

Using the cut side of a lemon to rub kosher salt over a cutting board will help to sterilize the board after it is used for cutting chicken. Hot, soapy water will also keep cutting surfaces bacteria-free.

3. Using a small, sharp knife, slit the membrane covering the breastbone and flex the breast upward to pop out the bone.

4. Pull or cut out the breastbone. Place the whole breast, skin side down, on the cutting board. Cut along the center of the whole breast to separate it into two halves.

Frying and Grilling

FRYING

1. Coat the chicken pieces with flour, breading, or batter, as directed in a recipe. Pour oil to a depth of 1 inch (2.5 cm) into a deep sauté or frying pan. Heat to 350°F (180°C) on a deep-frying thermometer, or until the corner of a piece of chicken sizzles upon contact with the oil.

2. Fry in batches, taking care not to crowd the pan, which would hinder the browning that seals in the juices. Use long tongs to turn the pieces until evenly browned on all sides. Complete the cooking on a baking sheet in the oven.

BASTING TIPS

Baste chicken regularly to help keep it moist when grilling, roasting, or broiling. Use a basting brush or, for an extra touch of flavor, a bundle of fresh herb sprigs (above). When basting with a marinade that has been used for raw chicken pieces, do not baste any later than 5 minutes before the chicken is done grilling.

INDIRECT-HEAT GRILLING

Use indirect heat when grilling chicken marinated in sweet or oil-based sauces prone to burning, or when grilling large pieces or whole birds for long periods. When the coals are ready, move them to the perimeter or one side of the grill before setting the grill rack in place.

Braising and Stewing

Good pans are a must for cooking chicken to perfection. For rapid browning and long cooking, choose heavy stainless steel, thick aluminum, cast iron, or heavy enamel.

These two moist cooking methods result in juicy and flavorful meat. First, the chicken pieces are browned to seal in the juices. Then they are removed and the pan is deglazed. The chicken is returned to the pan, liquid is added—less for braises than for stews—and the chicken is slowly cooked.

BROWNING

1. Spread plain or seasoned flour on a plate. One piece at a time, turn the chicken in the flour to coat it evenly. Shake off any excess and set aside.

2. Heat oil until a corner of a chicken piece sizzles when dipped into it. Add the chicken and cook until browned, turning with tongs.

DEGLAZING

If the recipe calls for it, sauté other flavorful ingredients in the pan. Add a liquid—here, stock—stirring to dislodge any bits from the pan bottom.

BRAISING OR STEWING

Return the chicken to the pan, add any other liquids, and bring to a boil. Reduce the heat, cover, and simmer gently until the chicken is done.

Chicken Stock

If you like, save vegetable and herb trimmings such as green onion, carrot, and celery tops and parsley stems for the stockpot. Do not add salt to the stock until it is used in a recipe; this allows you to season the recipe more accurately. For long-term storage, divide the defatted stock among 3 or 4 containers and freeze for up to 3 months.

4 lb (2 kg) chicken backs, necks, and wings
1 or 2 yellow onions, quartered
3 celery stalks including leaves, coarsely chopped
2 carrots, coarsely chopped
6 green (spring) onions or 1 leek, including tender green tops, coarsely chopped
1 tablespoon white wine vinegar or dry white wine
1 bay leaf, crushed
2 cloves garlic, crushed
4–6 peppercorns
¼ cup (⅓ oz/10 g) coarsely chopped fresh flat-leaf (Italian) parsley
1 fresh thyme sprig or 1 tablespoon fresh thyme leaves
1 tablespoon chopped fresh sage

✳ In a stockpot, combine all the ingredients and add water to cover by 1–2 inches (2.5–5 cm). Bring slowly to a boil over medium heat, skimming off any foam with a spoon or skimmer.

✳ Reduce the heat to medium-low and cover partially. Simmer gently, skimming as necessary, for 1½–2 hours. Remove from the heat. Using a slotted spoon, lift out the chicken pieces and discard. Strain through a fine-mesh sieve into a bowl. Let cool, then cover and immediately refrigerate for up to 5 days. Using a large spoon, lift off the fat that has solidified on top before using or freezing (see note).

MAKES ABOUT 3½ QT (3.5 L)

POACHING CHICKEN

When a recipe calls for cooked chicken and you have no leftovers on hand, poaching is often the best way to cook chicken in a hurry. It also results in particularly moist, tender meat.

To poach chicken, put it in a cooking vessel large and deep enough to hold it comfortably. A whole chicken should first be trussed (page 10). Add cold liquid to cover completely. Slowly bring to a boil, regularly skimming away any froth and scum that rise to the surface. Reduce the heat and simmer gently, skimming as necessary, until cooked through, 10–15 minutes for boneless, skinless chicken breasts or about 1 hour for a whole chicken.

Planning Menus

All of the recipes in this book have been designed to complement one another, giving you as many ways as possible to mix and match them to create menus that suit your tastes and the occasion. As you look through the recipes, however, certain obvious pairings may suggest themselves, based on the ingredients, seasonings, cuisines, or cooking styles. The ten menus shown here suggest just a few of the many possibilities. Keep in mind that even one or two thoughtfully selected dishes can make any meal special. Add a simple salad, a fresh vegetable, some steamed rice, or another easy dish of your own devising, and you'll have a menu guaranteed to make a lasting impression.

Harvest Supper

Beet and Walnut Salad
with Raspberry Vinaigrette
PAGE 24

Autumn Chicken Stew
with Chanterelles
PAGE 86

Tarte Tatin
PAGE 106

Garden Party

Frisée and Spinach Salad
PAGE 27

Chicken with Lemon,
Garlic, and Parsley
PAGE 64

Vegetable Gratin
PAGE 92

Almond-Fruit Tart
PAGE 98

Mexican Lunch

Potato, Corn,
and Avocado Chowder
PAGE 23

Chicken Fajitas
with Guacamole
PAGE 48

Tropical Fruit
in Citrus Syrup
PAGE 102

Casual Sunday Supper

Easy Barbecue

Springtime Celebration

Pan-Asian Celebration

Company's Coming

Warming Winter Repast

Dinner in Tuscany

Spicy Tomato Soup

PREP TIME: 25 MINUTES

COOKING TIME: 55 MINUTES

INGREDIENTS

2 tablespoons pure olive oil

1 yellow onion, finely chopped

1 carrot, peeled and grated

4 cloves garlic, chopped

¼ teaspoon cayenne pepper or a dash of hot-pepper sauce such as Tabasco, plus cayenne pepper for garnish

3 lb (1.5 kg) tomatoes, peeled, seeded, and chopped

1⅓ cups (11 fl oz/340 ml) Chicken Stock (*page 15*)

salt and ground black pepper to taste

½ cup (4 oz/125 g) plain yogurt

¼ cup (⅓ oz/10 g) minced fresh dill, flat-leaf (Italian) parsley, or snipped fresh chives

Cayenne or hot-pepper sauce adds a subtle touch of fire to this soup, while a garnish of yogurt contributes an enticing creaminess to counteract the heat.

SERVES 4–6

❋ In a saucepan over medium-high heat, warm the oil. Add the onion and carrot and sauté until softened, about 5 minutes. Add the garlic and ¼ teaspoon cayenne pepper or hot-pepper sauce and sauté until the garlic has softened, about 30 seconds. Add the tomatoes and stock and bring to a boil. Reduce the heat to medium and simmer, uncovered, until the flavors are blended, at least 20 minutes or for up to 45 minutes. The longer the mixture cooks, the smoother it will become.

❋ Working in batches, transfer the soup to a blender or food processor and purée until smooth. Alternatively, pass through a food mill placed over a bowl. Return to the saucepan over medium-high heat and season with salt and pepper. Heat to serving temperature.

❋ Ladle into warmed bowls and top each serving with a dollop of yogurt and a sprinkling of dill or other herb. Dust with cayenne pepper and serve immediately.

NUTRITIONAL ANALYSIS PER SERVING: Calories 146 (Kilojoules 613); Protein 5 g; Carbohydrates 19 g; Total Fat 7 g; Saturated Fat 1 g; Cholesterol 2 mg; Sodium 68 mg; Dietary Fiber 4 g

Hot-and-Sour Broth with Mushrooms

PREP TIME: 40 MINUTES, PLUS
30 MINUTES FOR SOAKING

COOKING TIME: 30 MINUTES

INGREDIENTS

1 oz (30 g) dried Chinese black
mushrooms

½ cup (4 fl oz/125 ml) boiling water

1 lemongrass stalk, white part only,
or grated zest of 1 lime

6 cups (48 fl oz/1.5 l) Chicken Stock
(page 15)

¼ cup (2 fl oz/60 ml) lime juice

1 tablespoon peeled and finely
chopped fresh ginger

2 teaspoons fish sauce

½–1 teaspoon chile paste with garlic
(see note)

1 cup (3 oz/90 g) thinly sliced fresh
oyster or cremini mushrooms

1 clove garlic, minced

2 teaspoons soy sauce

salt to taste

2 green (spring) onions, sliced on
the diagonal

Light and only mildly spicy, this simple broth is a suitable first course for nearly any Asian-inspired meal. Look for chile paste with garlic in well-stocked food stores and Asian markets.

SERVES 4

❈ Place the dried mushrooms in a small bowl and add the boiling water. Let stand until softened, about 30 minutes. Drain, reserving the liquid. Remove the stems and discard. Slice the caps. Strain the liquid through a sieve lined with cheesecloth (muslin). Set aside the sliced mushrooms and soaking liquid.

❈ If using the lemongrass, cut into 2-inch (5-cm) lengths and crush with the side of a knife.

❈ In a saucepan, combine the lemongrass or lime zest, stock, lime juice, ginger, fish sauce, and chile paste with garlic. Add the sliced reconstituted mushrooms and their soaking liquid. Bring to a boil over high heat. Reduce the heat to medium and simmer, uncovered, until the stock is infused with the seasonings, about 20 minutes.

❈ Using a slotted spoon, remove the lemongrass pieces and discard. Stir in the fresh mushrooms and garlic and cook until soft, about 5 minutes. Stir in the soy sauce and taste and adjust the seasonings with salt.

❈ Ladle into warmed bowls and garnish with the green onions. Serve immediately.

NUTRITIONAL ANALYSIS PER SERVING: Calories 82 (Kilojoules 344); Protein 6 g; Carbohydrates 11 g; Total Fat 2 g; Saturated Fat 1 g; Cholesterol 4 mg; Sodium 430 mg; Dietary Fiber 2 g

COOKING TIP: If fresh oyster or cremini mushrooms are unavailable, substitute fresh white mushrooms. To turn the broth into a main-course soup, cut 1 lb (500 g) skinless, boneless chicken into strips and simmer in the broth until opaque. Accompany with steamed rice.

Potato, Corn, and Avocado Chowder

PREP TIME: 30 MINUTES

COOKING TIME: 30 MINUTES

INGREDIENTS

2 tablespoons canola or safflower oil

I yellow onion, chopped

6 green (spring) onions, chopped

2 cloves garlic, minced

2 russet potatoes, about I lb (500 g)
   total weight, peeled if desired,
   and cubed

I garnet yam or sweet potato, about
   ½ lb (250 g), peeled and cubed

2 white rose or Yellow Finn potatoes,
   about I lb (500 g) total weight,
   peeled and cubed

8 cups (64 fl oz/2 l) Chicken Stock
   (page 15) or water

½ cup (¾ oz/20 g) chopped fresh
   cilantro (fresh coriander)

salt and ground white or black pepper
   to taste

1½ cups (9 oz/280 g) corn kernels
   (cut from about 3 ears)

I cup (8 fl oz/250 ml) milk or light
   (single) cream

I avocado, pitted, peeled, and
   chopped, tossed with 2 tablespoons lime juice

Inspired by Colombian *ajiaco,* this filling soup has an appealing
variety of textures.

SERVES 4–6

❀ In a saucepan over medium-high heat, warm the oil. Add the yellow
and green onions and sauté until softened, about 5 minutes. Stir in the
garlic and the russet potatoes, yam or sweet potato, and white rose or
Yellow Finn potatoes. Pour in the stock or water and add half of the
cilantro. Bring to a boil, reduce the heat to low, and simmer, uncovered,
until the potatoes are soft and the flavors are blended, about 20 minutes.
Season with salt and pepper.

❀ Add the corn and the milk or cream. Simmer until the corn is tender,
about 5 minutes longer; do not allow to boil. If you like, mash some of
the potatoes with a fork to thicken the soup.

❀ To serve, stir in the remaining cilantro and ladle the chowder into
warmed soup bowls. Top with the avocado, dividing evenly.

NUTRITIONAL ANALYSIS PER SERVING: Calories 434 (Kilojoules 1,823); Protein 13 g;
Carbohydrates 64 g; Total Fat 16 g; Saturated Fat 3 g; Cholesterol 12 mg; Sodium 191 mg;
Dietary Fiber 8 g

Beet and Walnut Salad with Raspberry Vinaigrette

PREP TIME: 40 MINUTES, PLUS
1 HOUR FOR MARINATING

COOKING TIME: 35 MINUTES

INGREDIENTS

3 beets, about ¾ lb (375 g) total weight

⅓ cup (3 fl oz/80 ml) extra-virgin olive oil

3 tablespoons raspberry vinegar

½ teaspoon dry mustard

salt and ground pepper to taste

1 clove garlic, lightly crushed and stuck onto the end of a toothpick

½ cup (2 oz/60 g) walnuts

2 heads Bibb or butter (Boston) lettuce, torn into bite-sized pieces

2–3 oz (60–90 g) Roquefort or other blue cheese, crumbled (optional)

Marinating the beets in the vinaigrette infuses them with flavor and intensifies the color of the dressing. The combination of colors and tastes makes a refreshing starter course. When you want only the mellow flavor of garlic in a vinaigrette, follow the method used here: lightly crush a clove, spear it with a toothpick, and place in the vinaigrette for at least 1 hour or as long as 12 hours.

SERVES 4–6

❊ Trim the stems from the beets, leaving about ½ inch (12 mm) intact; do not peel. Place the beets in a small saucepan, add water to cover, and bring to a boil. Reduce the heat to low, cover, and simmer until tender, about 20 minutes. Drain and, when cool enough to handle, cut off the stem and root ends and peel off the skins. Cut the beets into julienne strips and place in a bowl.

❊ Meanwhile, in a small bowl, whisk together the oil, vinegar, and mustard. Season with salt and pepper and add the garlic. Let stand for 30 minutes. (The dressing may be made to this point up to 12 hours in advance and refrigerated. Return to room temperature before continuing.)

❊ Preheat an oven to 350°F (180°C). Spread the walnuts on a baking sheet and toast until lightly colored and fragrant, 10–15 minutes. Remove from the oven and let cool.

❊ Remove the garlic from the dressing and discard. Pour the dressing over the beets and let stand for at least 1 hour at room temperature or for up to 2 days in the refrigerator. (If necessary, bring to room temperature before serving.)

❊ Just before serving, place the lettuce in a bowl. Using a slotted spoon, remove the beets from the dressing and place in another bowl. Drizzle the dressing over the lettuce and toss well to coat. Divide among individual plates. Top with the beets and garnish with the walnuts and the cheese, if using.

NUTRITIONAL ANALYSIS PER SERVING: Calories 240 (Kilojoules 1,008); Protein 4 g; Carbohydrates 10 g; Total Fat 22 g; Saturated Fat 3 g; Cholesterol 0 mg; Sodium 44 mg; Dietary Fiber 2 g

Frisée and Spinach Salad with Pancetta

PREP TIME: 20 MINUTES

COOKING TIME: 10 MINUTES

INGREDIENTS

1 oz (30 g) pancetta or other unsmoked bacon, minced

½ shallot, minced

⅓ cup (3 fl oz/80 ml) extra-virgin olive oil

2 tablespoons balsamic vinegar

1 teaspoon Dijon mustard

salt and ground pepper to taste

1 head frisée, torn into bite-sized pieces

½ bunch young, tender spinach, about 6 oz (185 g), tough stems removed

The success of this salad results from the balance it strikes among a variety of flavors: sweet and tangy from the balsamic vinegar, salty from the pancetta, and mildly bitter from the frisée. If frisée is unavailable, substitute chicory (curly endive), Belgian endive (chicory/witloof), or radicchio.

SERVES 4–6

✾ In a small, nonstick frying pan over medium heat, cook the pancetta, stirring often, until crisp, about 5 minutes. Pour off all the drippings. Stir in the shallot and sauté until softened, 1–2 minutes. Remove from the heat.

✾ In a small bowl, whisk together the oil, vinegar, and mustard. Season with salt and pepper.

✾ Place the frisée and spinach in a bowl. Drizzle with the vinaigrette and toss well, then sprinkle with the pancetta-shallot mixture and toss again. Serve immediately.

NUTRITIONAL ANALYSIS PER SERVING: Calories 170 (Kilojoules 714); Protein 3 g; Carbohydrates 4 g; Total Fat 17 g; Saturated Fat 3 g; Cholesterol 3 mg; Sodium 134 mg; Dietary Fiber 2 g

Three Bean and Corn Salad with Cider Vinaigrette

PREP TIME: 35 MINUTES, PLUS
3½ HOURS FOR SOAKING
AND MARINATING

COOKING TIME: 1 HOUR

INGREDIENTS

½ cup (3½ oz/105 g) dried red beans
   such as kidney

½ cup (3½ oz/105 g) dried cannellini
   or Great Northern beans

½ cup (3½ oz/105 g) dried black
   beans

1 cup (6 oz/185 g) corn kernels
   (cut from about 2 ears)

3 green (spring) onions, chopped

1 whole red bell pepper (capsicum) or
   ½ each red bell pepper and green
   bell pepper, seeded and chopped

⅓ cup (3 fl oz/80 ml) canola or
   safflower oil

¼ cup (2 fl oz/60 ml) tomato salsa

2–3 tablespoons cider vinegar

2 cloves garlic, minced

½ teaspoon ground cumin

salt and ground pepper to taste

½ cup (⅔ oz/20 g) chopped fresh
   cilantro (fresh coriander)

PREP TIP: To remove the kernels
from an ear of corn, hold the pointed
end and steady the stalk end on a
cutting board. Using a sturdy, sharp
knife, cut down along the ear to strip
off the kernels.

Tart and hearty, this filling bean salad makes a colorful companion
to simple grilled chicken, whether served at home or at a
summertime picnic. Cook each variety of bean separately to
ensure optimum texture and to maintain the color.

SERVES 6–8

✹ Pick over each variety of bean and discard any misshapen beans or
stones. Rinse each variety separately and drain. Place in separate bowls,
add plenty of water to cover, and let soak for 3 hours.

✹ Drain and place each variety in a saucepan with water to cover by
2 inches (5 cm). Bring to a boil, reduce the heat to low, and simmer,
uncovered, until tender, about 45 minutes for red beans, about 50 minutes for cannellini or Great Northern, and about 60 minutes for black
beans. Drain, rinse, and let cool. The cooking times will depend on the
type and age of the beans.

✹ Meanwhile, bring a small saucepan two-thirds full of water to a boil.
Add the corn kernels and blanch for about 2 minutes. Drain, rinse
with cold running water to halt the cooking, and drain again.

✹ In a bowl, combine all the beans with the corn, green onions, and
bell pepper. Mix well.

✹ In a small bowl, whisk together the oil, salsa, vinegar to taste, garlic,
and cumin. Season with salt and pepper. Pour over the bean mixture
and stir to mix. Let stand for at least 30 minutes or for up to 2 hours
to allow the flavors to blend.

✹ Just before serving, garnish with the cilantro.

NUTRITIONAL ANALYSIS PER SERVING: Calories 265 (Kilojoules 1,113); Protein 11 g;
Carbohydrates 33 g; Total Fat 11 g; Saturated Fat 1 g; Cholesterol 0 mg; Sodium 103 mg;
Dietary Fiber 10 g

Roast Chicken with Garlic and Herbs

PREP TIME: 20 MINUTES

COOKING TIME: 1½ HOURS

INGREDIENTS

1 chicken, 3½–4 lb (1.75–2 kg)

3 cloves garlic, minced

1 tablespoon paprika

2 teaspoons minced fresh marjoram

2 teaspoons minced fresh basil

2 teaspoons minced fresh chervil

2 teaspoons minced fresh rosemary

2 tablespoons pure olive oil

salt and ground pepper to taste

¾ cup (6 fl oz/180 ml) Chicken Stock (page 15)

¼ cup (2 fl oz/60 ml) dry white wine

1½ tablespoons all-purpose (plain) flour

The simplicity of roast chicken is elevated by a fresh herb paste tucked under the skin. The chicken is also good cold.

SERVES 4

❋ Preheat an oven to 425°F (220°C). Rinse the chicken and pat dry with paper towels.

❋ In a small bowl, combine the garlic, paprika, marjoram, basil, chervil, rosemary, and olive oil. Mix well with a fork to form a paste and season with salt and pepper. Using your fingers and beginning at the neck opening, gently loosen the skin on the breasts, thighs, and legs; be careful not to tear the skin. Again using your fingers, rub about three-fourths of the paste under the skin evenly over the breast, thigh, and leg meat. Gently pat the skin in place and then rub the skin of the entire bird with the remaining paste. Using kitchen string, tie the drumsticks together. Tuck the wing tips under the body. Place the chicken, breast side up, on a rack in a roasting pan.

❋ Place in the oven and immediately reduce the heat to 350°F (180°C). Roast until an instant-read thermometer inserted into the thickest part of the breast away from the bone registers 170°F (77°C) and in the thigh registers 185°F (85°C), or until the juice runs clear when the thigh is pierced, about 1¼ hours. Remove from the oven and transfer to a platter. Cover with aluminum foil and let stand for 5–10 minutes before carving.

❋ Meanwhile, pour the pan drippings from the roasting pan into a small saucepan. Skim the fat off the top. Place the roasting pan on the stove top over high heat. Add the stock and wine and deglaze the pan, stirring to remove any browned bits from the pan bottom. Remove from the heat. Place the saucepan holding the drippings over medium heat and add the flour. Cook, stirring, until beginning to brown, about 1½ minutes. Add the stock from the roasting pan, bring to a boil, and cook until reduced to the desired consistency, 5–10 minutes. Season with salt and pepper and pour into a warmed sauceboat.

❋ To serve, carve the chicken. Pass the gravy at the table.

NUTRITIONAL ANALYSIS PER SERVING: Calories 542 (Kilojoules 2,276); Protein 52 g; Carbohydrates 5 g; Total Fat 33 g; Saturated Fat 8 g; Cholesterol 165 mg; Sodium 171 mg; Dietary Fiber 0 g

Chicken in White Wine with Potatoes

PREP TIME: 20 MINUTES

COOKING TIME: 50 MINUTES

INGREDIENTS

4 tablespoons (1½ oz/45 g) all-purpose (plain) flour

½ teaspoon salt

½ teaspoon ground pepper

2 chicken breast halves, about ½ lb (250 g) each, skinned

2 chicken thighs, about 6 oz (185 g) each, skinned

2 chicken drumsticks, about ¼ lb (125 g) each, skinned

2 tablespoons pure olive oil

3 shallots, chopped

1 carrot, peeled and chopped

1 celery stalk, chopped

½ lb (250 g) fresh cremini mushrooms, brushed clean and quartered

2 cloves garlic, minced

1 teaspoon minced fresh thyme

2 cups (16 fl oz/500 ml) Sauvignon Blanc or other dry white wine

5 small new potatoes, quartered or halved

2 teaspoons unsalted butter, at room temperature

¼ cup (½ oz/15 g) chopped fresh flat-leaf (Italian) parsley

This dish is inspired by the famed *coq au vin* of the French kitchen, which is traditionally made with red wine. The addition of potatoes makes it a one-pot meal.

SERVES 4

❈ On a plate, stir together 3 tablespoons of the flour and the salt and pepper. Lightly coat both sides of each chicken piece with the flour mixture, shaking off the excess.

❈ In a wide frying pan over high heat, warm the oil. Add the chicken pieces in batches and sauté, turning once, until browned, about 2 minutes on each side. Transfer to a plate and set aside.

❈ Reduce the heat to medium, add the shallots, carrot, and celery, and sauté until softened, about 4 minutes. Stir in the mushrooms and sauté for 1–2 minutes longer. Then stir in the garlic and sprinkle in the thyme. Raise the heat to high, pour in the wine, and deglaze the pan, stirring to remove any browned bits from the pan bottom.

❈ Return the chicken to the pan and return to a boil. Add the potatoes and reduce the heat to medium-low. Cover and simmer until the chicken is opaque throughout and the juices run clear and the potatoes are tender, about 25 minutes.

❈ Meanwhile, in a small bowl, using your fingers, mix together the butter and the remaining 1 tablespoon flour to form a paste. When the chicken is ready, transfer the pieces to a warmed serving platter. Drop the paste into the sauce bit by bit, stirring to mix. Bring to a boil over high heat and cook, stirring, until the sauce is thickened, about 5 minutes.

❈ Spoon the sauce over the chicken, garnish with the parsley, and serve.

NUTRITIONAL ANALYSIS PER SERVING: Calories 432 (Kilojoules 1,814); Protein 38 g; Carbohydrates 39 g; Total Fat 13 g; Saturated Fat 3 g; Cholesterol 112 mg; Sodium 427 mg; Dietary Fiber 4 g

Chicken Sauté with Madeira Sauce

PREP TIME: 15 MINUTES

COOKING TIME: 20 MINUTES

INGREDIENTS

4 skinless, boneless chicken breast
halves, about 6 oz (185 g) each

2 tablespoons all-purpose (plain)
flour

1 tablespoon unsalted butter

1 tablespoon canola or safflower oil

salt and ground white or black
pepper to taste

1 cup (8 fl oz/250 ml) Chicken Stock
(page 15)

½ cup (4 fl oz/125 ml) Sauvignon
Blanc or other dry wine

⅓ cup (3 fl oz/80 ml) Madeira or
other sweet wine

2–4 tablespoons heavy (double)
cream

¼ cup (½ oz/15 g) chopped fresh
flat-leaf (Italian) parsley

COOKING TIP: For a rose-colored
sauce, substitute port for the Madeira.

The rich depth of sweet-tart Madeira marries perfectly with the light flavors of sautéed chicken breasts. The sauce gives the easy-to-prepare dish an elegance, making it a good candidate for a special dinner when you are pressed for time.

SERVES 4

❀ One at a time, place the chicken breasts between 2 sheets of plastic wrap and flatten with a meat pounder until an even ½ inch (12 mm) thick. Spread the flour on a plate, then lightly coat both sides of each breast with the flour, shaking off the excess.

❀ In a frying pan over high heat, melt the butter with the oil. Add the chicken breasts and sauté, turning once, until just beginning to brown, 1–2 minutes on each side. Transfer to a platter, season with salt and pepper, and set aside.

❀ Pour off any fat from the pan and return to high heat. Pour in the stock and deglaze the pan, stirring to remove any browned bits from the pan bottom. Bring to a boil, add the dry and sweet wines, and boil until reduced by half, about 5 minutes. Return the chicken to the pan and reduce the heat to medium. Cook, turning once or twice, until the chicken is opaque throughout and the juices run clear, about 5 minutes longer. Transfer the chicken to a warmed platter; keep warm.

❀ Stir the cream to taste into the pan juices and cook over medium-high heat just until slightly thickened, about 2 minutes. Pour over the chicken. Garnish with the parsley and serve.

NUTRITIONAL ANALYSIS PER SERVING: Calories 314 (Kilojoules 1,319); Protein 41 g; Carbohydrates 7 g; Total Fat 13 g; Saturated Fat 5 g; Cholesterol 122 mg; Sodium 141 mg; Dietary Fiber 0 g

Chicken Teriyaki

PREP TIME: 20 MINUTES

COOKING TIME: 15 MINUTES,
PLUS PREPARING FIRE

INGREDIENTS

½ cup (4 fl oz/125 ml) soy sauce

¼ cup (2 fl oz/60 ml) mirin

¼ cup (2 fl oz/60 ml) dry sake or
dry sherry

1 tablespoon peeled and chopped
fresh ginger

2 cloves garlic, minced

1 teaspoon brown sugar

4 skinless, boneless chicken breast
halves, about 6 oz (185 g) each

SERVING TIP: For a colorful presentation, garnish the chicken with 1 or 2 green (spring) onions, thinly sliced on the diagonal, and a sprinkling of black or white sesame seeds or a mixture of both.

Chicken takes on a beautiful mahogany finish when brushed with this Japanese-style glaze. The saltiness imparted by the soy sauce complements the smoky flavor from the fire. Using both mirin (sweet rice wine) and dry sake adds depth to the sauce.

SERVES 4

❀ Prepare a fire in a grill.

❀ In a small saucepan over high heat, combine the soy sauce, mirin, sake or sherry, ginger, garlic, and brown sugar. Stir well and bring to a boil. Boil for 1 minute, then remove from the heat, pour into a shallow bowl, and let cool completely.

❀ One at a time, place the chicken breasts between 2 sheets of plastic wrap and flatten with a meat pounder until an even ½ inch (12 mm) thick. Cover and refrigerate until needed.

❀ About 15 minutes before the fire is ready, scoop out and reserve about ½ cup (4 fl oz/125 ml) of the soy mixture to use for basting. Then, place the chicken breasts in the remaining cooled soy mixture.

❀ When the fire is hot, remove each chicken breast from the soy mixture and place on the grill rack directly over the fire. Discard any soy mixture remaining in the bowl. Grill, turning once and brushing with some of the reserved soy mixture, until the chicken is opaque throughout and the juices run clear, about 4 minutes on each side.

❀ Transfer the chicken to a serving platter, brush with the remaining reserved soy mixture, and serve.

NUTRITIONAL ANALYSIS PER SERVING: Calories 252 (Kilojoules 1,058); Protein 41 g; Carbohydrates 8 g; Total Fat 2 g; Saturated Fat 1 g; Cholesterol 99 mg; Sodium 1,675 mg; Dietary Fiber 0 g

Chicken Stir-Fry with Walnuts

PREP TIME: 20 MINUTES,
PLUS 15 MINUTES FOR
MARINATING

COOKING TIME: 10 MINUTES

INGREDIENTS

1 lb (500 g) skinless, boneless chicken
breasts

¼ cup (2 fl oz/60 ml) reduced-sodium
soy sauce

2 tablespoons mirin or sweet sherry

2 tablespoons seasoned rice vinegar

1 tablespoon peeled and minced
fresh ginger

2 cloves garlic, minced

2 tablespoons canola or safflower oil

½ cup (2 oz/60 g) walnut pieces

5 green (spring) onions, cut on the
diagonal into 1½-inch (4-cm)
lengths

1 cup (8 fl oz/250 ml) Chicken Stock
(page 15)

2 tablespoons cornstarch (cornflour)
dissolved in an additional 1 tablespoon stock or water

PREP TIP: Because stir-frying goes
very quickly, be sure to have all the
ingredients ready and close at hand
before you start cooking.

Put a pot of jasmine rice on the stove to cook while the chicken is marinating, and the chicken and the rice will be ready to serve at about the same time.

SERVES 4

❁ Cut the chicken breasts into slivers 1 inch (2.5 cm) long and ¼ inch (6 mm) wide. In a bowl, stir together soy sauce, mirin or sherry, vinegar, ginger, and garlic. Add the chicken and stir to mix well. Let stand at room temperature for at least 15 minutes or refrigerate for up to 1 hour.

❁ Place a wok or heavy frying pan over high heat. When the pan is hot, add the oil and swirl to coat the bottom and sides of the pan. Add the walnuts and toss and stir until the nuts begin to deepen in color, about 1 minute. Using a slotted spoon, transfer to a small plate.

❁ Add the green onions to the oil remaining in the pan and toss and stir just until their color brightens, about 30 seconds. Using the slotted spoon, transfer to another small plate. Leave the pan over high heat.

❁ Using the slotted spoon, lift the chicken from the marinade, reserving the marinade, and add the chicken to the pan. Toss and stir until opaque throughout, 1–2 minutes.

❁ Add the stock and the reserved marinade and bring to a boil. Quickly stir the cornstarch mixture and add to the pan along with the reserved green onions. Cook, stirring, until thickened, about 1 minute. Transfer to a warmed serving dish. Garnish with the reserved walnuts and serve at once.

NUTRITIONAL ANALYSIS PER SERVING: Calories 343 (Kilojoules 1,441); Protein 30 g; Carbohydrates 15 g; Total Fat 17 g; Saturated Fat 2 g; Cholesterol 67 mg; Sodium 848 mg; Dietary Fiber 1 g

Chicken in Coconut Milk

PREP TIME: 10 MINUTES

COOKING TIME: 30 MINUTES

INGREDIENTS

2 tablespoons canola or safflower oil

8 chicken thighs, about 6 oz (185 g)
    each, skinned

salt and ground white or black
    pepper to taste

1 shallot, finely chopped

1 red or green Thai chile, seeded
    and minced

1½ cups (12 fl oz/375 ml) coconut
    milk

1 teaspoon fish sauce (optional)

juice and grated zest of 1 lime

SERVING TIP: In addition to the
lime zest, garnish the chicken with a
confetti of ¼ cup (1½ oz/45 g) minced
red and/or green chiles or red and/or
green bell peppers (capsicums).

Coconut milk provides a cool, creamy balance to the heat of the minced chile in this Southeast Asian–inspired dish. Chicken thighs stand up to this preparation better than breasts, as they remain more succulent during the simmering.

SERVES 4

❈ In a heavy frying pan over high heat, warm the oil until very hot. Add the chicken and sauté, turning once, until browned, about 3 minutes on each side. Season to taste with salt and pepper.

❈ Reduce the heat to medium and add the shallot and chile. Standing back from the pan so you don't inhale the fumes from the chile, sauté until softened, about 1 minute. Stir in the coconut milk, fish sauce (if using), and lime juice. Bring to a boil, reduce the heat to low, and simmer uncovered, turning the chicken occasionally, until the chicken is opaque throughout and the sauce has thickened, about 20 minutes.

❈ Using tongs, transfer the chicken thighs to a warmed serving dish or individual plates. Spoon the sauce over the top. Garnish with the lime zest and serve.

NUTRITIONAL ANALYSIS PER SERVING: Calories 464 (Kilojoules 1,949); Protein 40 g; Carbohydrates 4 g; Total Fat 32 g; Saturated Fat 18 g; Cholesterol 161 mg; Sodium 178 mg; Dietary Fiber 0 g

Harvesttime Chicken and Peppers

PREP TIME: 15 MINUTES

COOKING TIME: 45 MINUTES

INGREDIENTS

6 tablespoons (2¼ oz/67 g) all-purpose (plain) flour

4 chicken breast halves, about ½ lb (250 g) each, skinned

4 chicken thighs, about 6 oz (185 g) each, skinned

4 chicken drumsticks, about ¼ lb (125 g) each, skinned

2 tablespoons pure olive oil

salt and ground white or black pepper to taste

1 yellow onion, halved and sliced

½ red bell pepper (capsicum), seeded and sliced crosswise

½ green bell pepper (capsicum), seeded and sliced crosswise

½ yellow bell pepper (capsicum), seeded and sliced crosswise

2 cloves garlic, minced

1 tablespoon minced fresh basil

1 tablespoon minced fresh oregano

1 tablespoon minced fresh flat-leaf (Italian) parsley

3 cups (18 oz/560 g) peeled, seeded, and chopped tomatoes

1 cup (8 fl oz/250 ml) Chicken Stock (*page 15*)

½ cup (4 fl oz/125 ml) Sauvignon Blanc or other dry white wine

Make this quick and colorful main course in summer or early fall when bell peppers are piled high in the market. For a variation, add ½ pound (250 g) shrimp (prawns), peeled and deveined, stirring them in about 5 minutes before the chicken is done.

SERVES 6

❋ Preheat an oven to 350°F (180°C).

❋ Spread the flour on a plate, then lightly coat both sides of each chicken piece with the flour, shaking off the excess.

❋ In a frying pan over high heat, warm the olive oil. Add the chicken in batches and sauté, turning once, until lightly browned, about 2 minutes on each side. Transfer to a baking dish large enough to hold all the chicken in a single layer. Repeat until all the chicken is browned, then season with salt and pepper and set aside.

❋ Reduce the heat to medium and add the onion, bell peppers, garlic, basil, oregano, and parsley. Sauté until softened, about 5 minutes. Stir in the tomatoes, stock, and wine, raise the heat to high, and bring to a boil. Pour the sauce evenly over the chicken.

❋ Cover and bake until the chicken is opaque throughout and the juices run clear, 20–30 minutes.

❋ Uncover and serve hot directly from the dish.

NUTRITIONAL ANALYSIS PER SERVING: Calories 343 (Kilojoules 1,441); Protein 46 g; Carbohydrates 15 g; Total Fat 10 g; Saturated Fat 2 g; Cholesterol 143 mg; Sodium 180 mg; Dietary Fiber 2 g

Red-Hot Barbecued Chicken

PREP TIME: 30 MINUTES

COOKING TIME: 45 MINUTES,
    PLUS PREPARING FIRE

INGREDIENTS

FOR THE SAUCE

½ yellow onion, chopped

2 cloves garlic, minced

1 cup (8 fl oz/250 ml) tomato
    ketchup

⅓ cup (3 fl oz/80 ml) red wine vinegar

¼ cup (2 oz/60 g) firmly packed
    brown sugar

1 tablespoon prepared yellow
    mustard

1–2 teaspoons hot-pepper sauce
    such as Tabasco

1 teaspoon Worcestershire sauce

FOR THE SEASONING RUB

2 cloves garlic, minced

1½ teaspoons paprika

1 teaspoon salt

1 teaspoon cayenne pepper

½ teaspoon ground black pepper

2 chicken breast halves, about ½ lb
    (250 g) each, skinned

2 chicken thighs, about 6 oz (185 g)
    each, skinned

2 chicken drumsticks, about ¼ lb
    (125 g) each, skinned

2 chicken wings

Evocative of southern barbecue in Tennessee, Mississippi, and Georgia, this sweet-hot sauce is a perfect partner to chicken. The sauce can be made in advance and stored tightly covered in the refrigerator for up to 2 weeks.

SERVES 4

❊ Prepare an indirect-heat fire in a covered grill (see page 13).

❊ Meanwhile, make the sauce: In a small saucepan over medium-high heat, combine the onion, garlic, ketchup, vinegar, brown sugar, mustard, hot-pepper sauce, and Worcestershire sauce. Bring to a boil, stirring often. Reduce the heat to low and simmer, uncovered, until the sauce is thick and the flavors are blended, about 15 minutes. Remove from the heat and let cool.

❊ To make the seasoning rub, in a small bowl, stir together the garlic, paprika, salt, cayenne pepper, and black pepper. Rub the mixture on the chicken pieces, coating evenly, and set aside until ready to grill.

❊ When the fire is hot, place the chicken on the perimeter of the grill rack directly over the fire. Grill, turning once, until seared on both sides with grill marks, about 2 minutes on each side. Transfer the chicken pieces to a large platter and spoon the sauce evenly over them. Return the chicken to the grill rack, positioning the pieces in the center of the grill rack so that they are not directly over the fire. Cover the grill, open the vents halfway, and cook, turning once, until the chicken is opaque throughout and the juices run clear, about 20 minutes for the breasts and wings and 25 minutes for the thighs and drumsticks.

❊ Transfer the chicken pieces to a serving platter and serve at once.

NUTRITIONAL ANALYSIS PER SERVING: Calories 369 (Kilojoules 1,550); Protein 39 g; Carbohydrates 35 g; Total Fat 8 g; Saturated Fat 2 g; Cholesterol 125 mg; Sodium 1,477 mg; Dietary Fiber 2 g

Baked Spanish Rice with Chicken, Shrimp, and Mussels

PREP TIME: 15–20 MINUTES

COOKING TIME: 40 MINUTES

INGREDIENTS

1 bay leaf

½ cup (1 oz/30 g) chopped celery leaves

¼ yellow onion, plus 1 yellow onion, chopped

1 teaspoon salt, plus salt to taste

1 whole chicken breast, about 1 lb (500 g), skinned

1 cup (5 oz/155 g) shelled peas

2 cups (14 oz/440 g) long-grain white rice

2 tablespoons pure olive oil

1 green bell pepper (capsicum), seeded and chopped

3 cloves garlic, minced

3½ cups (28 fl oz/875 ml) Chicken Stock (page 15) or water

1 cup (8 fl oz/250 ml) tomato sauce

1 tablespoon chopped fresh oregano

3 saffron threads

ground pepper to taste

1–2 lb (500 g–1 kg) mussels, well scrubbed and debearded

½ cup (4 fl oz/125 ml) dry white wine or water

2 cups (16 fl oz/500 ml) water

½ lb (250 g) medium-sized shrimp (prawns), peeled and deveined

½ cup (¾ oz/20 g) chopped fresh flat-leaf (Italian) parsley

This dish, inspired by Spain's famed paella, combines rice and chicken, which are baked in the oven, with seafood, which is cooked on top of the stove.

SERVES 4–6

❋ Fill a saucepan two-thirds full with water. Add the bay leaf, celery leaves, ¼ onion, and 1 teaspoon salt. Bring to a boil, add the chicken, and reduce the heat to medium. Simmer, uncovered, until opaque through-out, about 15 minutes. Transfer the chicken to a plate, let cool, remove the meat from the bones, and cube. Strain the cooking liquid and reserve for another use.

❋ Meanwhile, bring another saucepan three-fourths full of water to a boil. Add the peas and boil until barely tender, 2–3 minutes. Rinse with cold running water to halt the cooking, drain, and set aside.

❋ Preheat an oven to 350°F (180°C). Oil or butter a shallow 2-qt (2-l) baking dish. Rinse the rice, changing the water until it runs clear. In a frying pan over medium-high heat, warm the oil. Add the chopped onion and bell pepper and sauté until softened, about 3 minutes. Stir in the garlic and sauté until fragrant, about 20 seconds longer. Stir in the rice and sauté for about 2 minutes. Add the stock or water, tomato sauce, oregano, and saffron. Season with salt and pepper and stir well. Bring to a boil and pour into the prepared baking dish.

❋ Cover and bake for 20 minutes. Remove from the oven, uncover, and stir in the cooked chicken and peas. Re-cover, return the dish to the oven, and continue baking until the rice is tender and all the liquid is absorbed, 10–15 minutes longer.

❋ Meanwhile, prepare the seafood: In a wide saucepan over medium-high heat, combine the mussels and wine or water, discarding any mussels that do not close to the touch. Cover and bring to a boil. Cook until the mussels open and are cooked through, 5–8 minutes. Remove from the heat and discard any mussels that did not open; keep warm. In another saucepan, bring the water to a boil over high heat. Add the shrimp and cook until they turn pink, about 3 minutes. Drain and keep warm.

❋ Remove the rice from the oven and uncover. Arrange the mussels and shrimp on top, sprinkle with the parsley, and serve.

NUTRITIONAL ANALYSIS PER SERVING: Calories 804 (Kilojoules 3,377); Protein 41 g; Carbohydrates 131 g; Total Fat 10 g; Saturated Fat 2 g; Cholesterol 104 mg; Sodium 1,017 mg; Dietary Fiber 5 g

Chicken Fajitas with Guacamole

PREP TIME: 25 MINUTES

COOKING TIME: 15 MINUTES

INGREDIENTS

FOR THE GUACAMOLE

I avocado, pitted and peeled

2 tablespoons lime or lemon juice

¼ cup (⅓ oz/10 g) chopped fresh
    cilantro (fresh coriander)

I green (spring) onion, chopped

I serrano chile, seeded and minced

I clove garlic, minced

8–12 corn or flour tortillas

2 tablespoons canola or safflower oil

I lb (500 g) skinless, boneless chicken
    breasts, cut into thin strips

I yellow onion, halved and sliced

½ red bell pepper (capsicum), seeded
    and sliced

½ green bell pepper (capsicum),
    seeded and sliced

I jalapeño or Anaheim chile, seeded,
    if desired, and finely chopped

2 teaspoons chopped fresh oregano

½ teaspoon ground cumin

2 cloves garlic, minced

2 tablespoons plus ¾ cup (6 fl oz/
    180 ml) tomato salsa

½ cup (4 fl oz/125 ml) water

2 plum (Roma) tomatoes, seeded
    and chopped

salt and ground pepper to taste

Leftover chicken can be substituted for the uncooked chicken. Stir it in after all the other ingredients are cooked and then heat through before serving.

SERVES 4

❀ Preheat an oven to 350°F (180°C).

❀ To make the guacamole, in a small bowl, mash the avocado with a fork. Add the lime or lemon juice, cilantro, green onion, serrano chile, and garlic. Mix well and set aside.

❀ Wrap the tortillas in aluminum foil and place in the oven to warm, about 10 minutes.

❀ Meanwhile, in a frying pan over medium-high heat, warm the oil. Add the chicken and sauté until opaque and firm, about 4 minutes. Using a slotted spoon, transfer the chicken to a plate and set aside.

❀ Add the onion and red and green bell peppers to the oil remaining in the pan and sauté over medium-high heat until softened, about 4 minutes. Stir in the chile, oregano, cumin, and garlic and sauté until the garlic is softened, about 20 seconds. Stir in the 2 tablespoons salsa and the water and bring to a boil. Add the tomatoes and season with salt and pepper. Cook, uncovered, until the liquid evaporates, about 5 minutes. Return the chicken to the pan, mix well, and heat to serving temperature. Transfer to a warmed serving platter.

❀ To serve, remove the tortillas from the oven and place the remaining ¾ cup (6 fl oz/180 ml) salsa in a small bowl. Set the chicken, tortillas, guacamole, and salsa on the table and let diners assemble their own filled tortillas.

NUTRITIONAL ANALYSIS PER SERVING: Calories 547 (Kilojoules 2,297); Protein 35 g; Carbohydrates 54 g; Total Fat 21 g; Saturated Fat 3 g; Cholesterol 66 mg; Sodium 979 mg; Dietary Fiber 5 g

Pasta with Chicken Meatballs

PREP TIME: 20 MINUTES

COOKING TIME: 40 MINUTES

INGREDIENTS

I red bell pepper (capsicum)

¼ cup (1½ oz/45 g) pine nuts

1½ lb (750 g) ground (minced) chicken

I yellow onion, finely chopped

2 oz (60 g) prosciutto, minced

2 cloves garlic, minced

2 teaspoons finely chopped fresh oregano

2 teaspoons finely chopped fresh basil

2 teaspoons finely chopped fresh rosemary

I egg

⅓–½ cup (1½–2 oz/45–60 g) fine dried bread crumbs

⅓ cup (½ oz/15 g) chopped fresh flat-leaf (Italian) parsley

salt and ground pepper to taste

2 tablespoons pure olive oil

3½ cups (28 fl oz/875 ml) canned crushed tomatoes

¾ lb (375 g) penne or ziti

½ cup (2 oz/60 g) grated Parmesan cheese

SERVING TIP: You can also serve the meatballs as appetizers, setting out toothpicks for spearing them, and re-serve the sauce for tossing with pasta.

Flavored with prosciutto and punctuated with pine nuts, these light meatballs are delicious served over a robust-shaped pasta such as penne or ziti.

SERVES 4

❀ Preheat a broiler (griller). Cut the bell pepper in half lengthwise and remove the seeds. Place, cut sides down, on a baking sheet. Broil (grill) until the skins blacken and blister. Remove from the broiler, drape the pepper loosely with aluminum foil, and let cool for 10 minutes, then peel away the skins. Transfer to a blender or food processor and purée until smooth. Set aside.

❀ In a small, nonstick frying pan over medium heat, toast the pine nuts, shaking the pan occasionally, until lightly browned, about 3 minutes. Transfer to a small plate and let cool.

❀ In a bowl, combine the chicken and half of the onion. Add the prosciutto, garlic, oregano, basil, rosemary, and egg and mix well with your hands. Add enough of the bread crumbs to bind the mixture. Mix in the parsley and toasted pine nuts, and season with salt and pepper. Pinch off walnut-sized pieces and roll into balls.

❀ In a frying pan over medium-high heat, warm the olive oil. Add the meatballs in batches and cook, turning as needed, until well browned on all sides, about 5 minutes. Transfer to a plate. Pour off all but 1 table-spoon of the fat from the pan and place over medium-high heat. Add the remaining onion and sauté until softened, about 2 minutes. Return the meatballs to the pan and add the tomatoes and red pepper purée. Bring to a boil, reduce the heat to medium-low, cover, and simmer until the meatballs are cooked through, about 20 minutes.

❀ Meanwhile, bring a large saucepan three-fourths full of water to a boil over high heat. Add the pasta, stir well, and cook until al dente (tender but firm to the bite), 10–12 minutes or according to the package directions. Drain and place in a warmed serving bowl.

❀ Ladle the meatballs and sauce over the pasta and serve. Pass the Parmesan at the table.

NUTRITIONAL ANALYSIS PER SERVING: Calories 910 (Kilojoules 3,822); Protein 59 g; Carbohydrates 90 g; Total Fat 36 g; Saturated Fat 9 g; Cholesterol 217 mg; Sodium 1,139 mg; Dietary Fiber 7 g

Flemish Chicken with Dried Fruit

PREP TIME: 25 MINUTES

COOKING TIME: 45 MINUTES

INGREDIENTS

½ cup (4 fl oz/125 ml) brandy, warmed

1 cup (6 oz/185 g) chopped dried fruit such as apricots, apples, raisins, or pitted prunes, or a combination

6 tablespoons (2¼ oz/67 g) all-purpose (plain) flour

2 chicken breast halves, about ½ lb (250 g) each, skinned

4 chicken thighs, about 6 oz (185 g) each, skinned

4 chicken drumsticks, about ¼ lb (125 g) each, skinned

1 lb (500 g) chicken wings

2 tablespoons canola or safflower oil

1 tablespoon unsalted butter

salt and ground pepper to taste

1 yellow onion, chopped

1 leek, white part only, chopped (optional)

3 cloves garlic, minced

2 or 3 new potatoes, cubed

1 teaspoon dried thyme

2 cups (16 fl oz/500 ml) Chicken Stock (page 15)

1 cup (8 fl oz/250 ml) Sauvignon Blanc or other dry white wine

The Flanders region of Belgium is home to this delectable stew, originally made with rabbit. It has a sweet-tart flavor due to the combination of dried fruit and wine. Although a single fruit can be used, a variety of dried fruits ensures a more complex flavor.

SERVES 4–6

✤ In a small bowl, pour the brandy over the fruit and let stand until rehydrated, 15–20 minutes.

✤ Meanwhile, spread the flour on a plate, then lightly coat both sides of each chicken piece with the flour, shaking off the excess.

✤ In a dutch oven or other large pot over high heat, warm the oil with the butter. Add the chicken pieces in batches and cook, turning once, until browned, about 2 minutes on each side. Transfer to a plate, season with salt and pepper, and set aside.

✤ Pour off all but 2 tablespoons of the fat from the pot. Place over medium-high heat, add the onion and the leek, if using, and sauté until softened, about 2 minutes. Stir in the garlic and sauté until softened, about 20 seconds. Add the potatoes and thyme. Raise the heat to high, pour in the stock and wine, and deglaze the pot, stirring to remove any browned bits from the bottom. Stir in the rehydrated fruit and brandy, return the chicken to the pot, reduce the heat to medium-low, and simmer, uncovered, until the chicken is opaque throughout and the juices run clear, about 25 minutes.

✤ If the sauce is too thin when the chicken is ready, transfer the chicken pieces to a warmed serving platter and keep warm. Raise the heat to high and boil the sauce until reduced to the desired consistency. Spoon the sauce over the chicken and serve immediately.

NUTRITIONAL ANALYSIS PER SERVING: Calories 442 (Kilojoules 1,856); Protein 35 g; Carbohydrates 49 g; Total Fat 12 g; Saturated Fat 4 g; Cholesterol 108 mg; Sodium 158 mg; Dietary Fiber 4 g

Chicken and Dumplings

PREP TIME: 30 MINUTES

COOKING TIME: 1¼ HOURS

INGREDIENTS

1 chicken, 3½–4 lb (1.75–2 kg)

2 celery stalks, chopped

2 carrots, peeled and sliced

1 green bell pepper (capsicum), seeded and chopped

1 rutabaga, peeled and cubed

1 parsnip, peeled and cubed

1 yellow onion, chopped

3 cloves garlic, minced

1 bay leaf

2 teaspoons salt

1 teaspoon dried thyme

½ teaspoon ground pepper

FOR THE DUMPLINGS

1 cup (5 oz/155 g) all-purpose (plain) flour

1½ teaspoons baking powder

½ teaspoon salt

3 tablespoons unsalted butter

¼ cup (⅓ oz/10 g) finely chopped flat-leaf (Italian) parsley

¼ cup (2 fl oz/60 ml) milk

Here is a traditional American Sunday dinner that couldn't be easier to prepare. A potful of chicken and vegetables topped with plump dumplings is comfort food at its best.

SERVES 4–6

❊ Place the whole chicken, breast side up, in a dutch oven or other large pot. Add the celery, carrots, bell pepper, rutabaga, parsnip, onion, garlic, bay leaf, salt, thyme, and pepper, distributing the vegetables and seasonings evenly around and over the chicken. Add water just to cover. Bring to a boil over high heat. Reduce the heat to medium-low, cover, and simmer until the chicken is opaque throughout and the juices run clear and the vegetables are tender, about 50 minutes.

❊ While the chicken is cooking, make the dumpling dough: In a bowl, stir together the flour, baking powder, and salt. Add the butter and, using a pastry blender or your fingers, work in the butter until the mixture resembles coarse crumbs. Add the parsley. Using a fork, stir in the milk until a firm dough forms. Pinch off pieces of dough and roll into balls. You should have enough dough for 8–10 dumplings.

❊ When the chicken is ready, using tongs, transfer it to a cutting board or platter and cover loosely with aluminum foil to keep warm.

❊ Raise the heat under the pot to medium-high. Bring the broth to a boil, skimming off any foam that rises to the surface. Using a slotted spoon, lower the dumplings into the boiling broth. Cover and cook until the dumplings puff and the interiors are uniformly set, 10–15 minutes. To test, cut into the center of a dumpling.

❊ Carve the chicken into serving pieces and transfer to individual bowls. Using a slotted spoon, place 1 or 2 dumplings and some of the vegetables into each bowl. Ladle the broth into the bowls and serve.

NUTRITIONAL ANALYSIS PER SERVING: Calories 454 (Kilojoules 1,907); Protein 41 g; Carbohydrates 43 g; Total Fat 13 g; Saturated Fat 6 g; Cholesterol 135 mg; Sodium 1,425 mg; Dietary Fiber 6 g

Chicken Sauté with Artichokes

PREP TIME: 30 MINUTES

COOKING TIME: 40 MINUTES

INGREDIENTS

I lemon, halved

I lb (500 g) small artichokes

3 tablespoons all-purpose (plain) flour

2 chicken breast halves, about ½ lb (250 g) each, skinned

2 chicken thighs, about 6 oz (185 g) each, skinned

2 chicken drumsticks, about ¼ lb (125 g) each, skinned

2 tablespoons pure olive oil

salt and ground white or black pepper to taste

4 cloves garlic, cut into slivers

I shallot, cut into slivers

I tablespoon minced fresh basil

I tablespoon minced fresh tarragon

I tablespoon minced fresh chervil

I tablespoon Dijon mustard

I cup (8 fl oz/250 ml) Sauvignon Blanc or other dry white wine

½ cup (4 fl oz/125 ml) Chicken Stock *(page 15)*

2 or 3 plum (Roma) tomatoes, seeded and chopped

¼ cup (½ oz/15 g) chopped fresh flat-leaf (Italian) parsley

Fresh artichokes taste best in this dish. If they are unavailable, use about 1½ cups (12 oz/375 g) thawed, frozen hearts or drained, marinated hearts and add them with the tomatoes.

SERVES 4–6

❈ Have ready a bowl three-fourths full of water to which you have added the juice from ½ lemon. Working with 1 artichoke at a time, cut off the stem even with the base. Cut off the top third of the artichoke. Starting at the base, break off 3 or 4 rows of the tough outer leaves, snapping them downward, until you reach the tender, pale green inner leaves. Trim away any dark green areas around the base. As you work, rub the cut surfaces with the remaining lemon half to prevent darkening. When the artichoke is fully trimmed, cut in half lengthwise and, using a sharp spoon or knife, scoop out and discard the prickly choke. Then cut each half in half again to create quarters and add to the lemon water. Set aside.

❈ Spread the flour on a plate, then lightly coat both sides of each chicken piece with the flour, shaking off the excess. In a frying pan over high heat, warm the oil. Add the chicken pieces and sauté, turning once, until lightly browned, 1–2 minutes on each side. Transfer to a platter, season with salt and pepper, and set aside.

❈ Pour off all but 2 tablespoons of the fat from the pan. Reduce the heat to medium, add the garlic and shallot, and sauté until softened, 1–2 minutes. Stir in the herbs and mustard. Raise the heat to high, pour in the wine and stock, and deglaze the pan, stirring to remove any browned bits from the pan bottom. Return the chicken to the pan and add the tomatoes. Reduce the heat to medium-high and cook until the chicken is opaque throughout and the juices run clear, about 20 minutes for the breasts and 30 minutes for the thighs and drumsticks, turning the chicken occasionally to ensure even cooking. About 10 minutes before the chicken is done, drain the artichokes and add to the pan. Transfer the chicken pieces to a plate as they are done, then just before the remaining chicken is done, return the cooked pieces to the pan to warm briefly.

❈ Transfer the contents of the pan to a warmed serving platter and garnish with the parsley. Serve at once.

NUTRITIONAL ANALYSIS PER SERVING: Calories 250 (Kilojoules 1,050); Protein 29 g; Carbohydrates 12 g; Total Fat 9 g; Saturated Fat 2 g; Cholesterol 86 mg; Sodium 231 mg; Dietary Fiber 3 g

Chicken Lasagne with Three Cheeses

PREP TIME: 25 MINUTES

COOKING TIME: 1¼ HOURS

INGREDIENTS

½ lb (250 g) dried lasagne noodles

1 teaspoon salt, plus salt to taste

2 tablespoons olive oil

1 lb (500 g) ground (minced) chicken or finely chopped skinned thigh meat

1 large yellow onion, finely chopped

1 red bell pepper (capsicum), seeded and finely chopped

3 cloves garlic, minced

½ teaspoon cayenne pepper

3 lb (1.5 kg) tomatoes, peeled, seeded, and chopped

2 tablespoons chopped fresh basil

ground pepper to taste

2 cups (1 lb/500 g) part-skim ricotta cheese

½ cup (2 oz/60 g) grated Parmesan or pecorino cheese

1 egg

½ cup (¾ oz/20 g) chopped fresh flat-leaf (Italian) parsley

½ lb (250 g) mozzarella cheese, shredded

Traditional lasagne is made a little spicy in this recipe. A hint of cayenne pepper brightens the fresh tomato sauce that is cooked with chicken and layered with pasta and a cooling mixture of ricotta, Parmesan, and mozzarella cheeses.

SERVES 4–6

❀ Bring a large pot three-fourths full of water to a boil. Add the lasagne noodles and the 1 teaspoon salt, stir well, and cook until almost tender, about 8 minutes. Drain and rinse in cool water. Lay the noodles flat on a kitchen towel and reserve.

❀ Preheat an oven to 350°F (180°C). Oil a 7-by-11-inch (18-by-28-cm) baking dish.

❀ In a frying pan over medium-high heat, warm the oil. Add the chicken and cook, stirring, until browned, about 6 minutes. Add the onion and bell pepper and sauté until softened, about 2 minutes. Stir in the garlic and cayenne pepper and sauté until the garlic is softened, about 20 seconds. Add the tomatoes and basil, stir well, and bring to a boil. Reduce the heat to low and simmer until thickened, about 20 minutes. Season with salt and pepper. Remove from the heat.

❀ In a bowl, combine the ricotta, Parmesan or pecorino cheese, and egg and mix well. Stir in the parsley.

❀ Line the bottom of the prepared baking dish with about one-fourth of the lasagne noodles, arranging them in a single layer and cutting as needed to fit. Spread with one-third of the ricotta mixture, sprinkle with one-third of the mozzarella, and then spoon on one-fourth of the sauce. Repeat the layering two more times, using up all of the ricotta mixture and the mozzarella. Top with the remaining noodles and finally the remaining sauce.

❀ Cover and bake until heated through and the sauce is bubbling, about 45 minutes. Remove from the oven and let stand for 10 minutes. Uncover and cut into squares to serve.

NUTRITIONAL ANALYSIS PER SERVING: Calories 762 (Kilojoules 3,200); Protein 50 g; Carbohydrates 58 g; Total Fat 37 g; Saturated Fat 16 g; Cholesterol 190 mg; Sodium 764 mg; Dietary Fiber 6 g

Fried Chicken with Herbs

PREP TIME: 45 MINUTES, PLUS 1¼ HOURS FOR SOAKING AND CHILLING

COOKING TIME: 1 HOUR

INGREDIENTS

2 chicken breast halves, about ½ lb (250 g) each, skinned

2 chicken thighs, about 6 oz (185 g) each, skinned

2 chicken drumsticks, about ¼ lb (125 g) each, skinned

2 chicken wings

1½ cups (12 fl oz/375 ml) buttermilk

1 egg

¾ cup (4 oz/125 g) all-purpose (plain) flour

¾ cup (3 oz/90 g) fine dried bread crumbs

2 cloves garlic, minced

1 tablespoon finely chopped fresh basil

1 tablespoon finely chopped fresh marjoram

1 teaspoon paprika

1 teaspoon salt

½ teaspoon ground pepper

canola oil for frying

2 tablespoons chopped fresh flat-leaf (Italian) parsley

An updated version of a traditional Sunday favorite, this fried chicken is browned in oil and finished in a hot oven.

SERVES 4

❀ Place the chicken pieces in a bowl with 1 cup (8 fl oz/250 ml) of the buttermilk. Cover and refrigerate for at least 1 hour or for up to 18 hours.

❀ Preheat an oven to 400°F (200°C).

❀ In a shallow bowl, beat the egg with a fork until blended, then beat in the remaining ½ cup (4 fl oz/125 ml) buttermilk. On a plate, mix together the flour, bread crumbs, garlic, basil, marjoram, paprika, salt, and pepper.

❀ Using tongs, lift the chicken pieces from the buttermilk, one at a time, and dip first into the flour mixture, coating evenly, and then into the egg mixture. Dip each piece again into the flour mixture and set aside on a baking sheet. When all the chicken pieces are coated, refrigerate them for 15 minutes while the oil heats.

❀ In a deep frying pan over high heat, pour in oil to a depth of 1 inch (2.5 cm). Heat the oil to 350°F (180°C) on a deep-frying thermometer, or until the corner of a piece of chicken dipped into the hot oil sizzles immediately upon contact. Working in batches, fry the chicken pieces, turning as needed, until well browned on all sides, about 10 minutes total. Do not crowd the pan. As soon as the pieces are browned, transfer them to a clean baking sheet.

❀ When all of the pieces are browned, place in the oven and bake until opaque throughout and the juices run clear, 20–30 minutes. The timing will depend upon the pieces; breasts will take the shorter time, while thighs and drumsticks will take longer. As the quicker-cooking pieces are done, transfer them to a plate.

❀ Arrange all the pieces on a serving platter and serve warm or at room temperature, garnished with the chopped parsley.

NUTRITIONAL ANALYSIS PER SERVING: Calories 576 (Kilojoules 2,419); Protein 47 g; Carbohydrates 38 g; Total Fat 25 g; Saturated Fat 4 g; Cholesterol 182 mg; Sodium 972 mg; Dietary Fiber 2 g

Chicken Kabobs with Lemon and Oregano

PREP TIME: 20 MINUTES, PLUS
1 HOUR FOR MARINATING

COOKING TIME: 20 MINUTES,
PLUS PREPARING FIRE

INGREDIENTS

½ cup (4 fl oz/125 ml) lemon juice

¼ cup (2 fl oz/60 ml) dry white wine

2 tablespoons pure olive oil

2 cloves garlic, minced

2 tablespoons chopped fresh
  oregano

grated zest of ½ lemon

salt and ground pepper to taste

1½ lb (750 g) skinless, boneless
  chicken breasts or thighs, cut into
  1½-inch (4-cm) cubes

1 Asian (slender) eggplant (aubergine),
  cut crosswise into slices

1 red bell pepper (capsicum), seeded
  and cut into 1-inch (2.5-cm)
  squares

1 yellow onion, halved, separated
  into layers, and then cut into
  1½-inch (4-cm) squares

1 lemon, cut into 8 wedges

COOKING TIP: For extra flavor, tie
together branches of oregano, rosemary, and thyme and use as a brush
for basting.

Cubes of chicken are threaded onto skewers with pieces
of eggplant, bell pepper, and onion and then brushed with
characteristic seasonings of the Greek Isles. Serve on a bed of
Perfect Pilaf (page 96) and garnish, if you like, with a sprinkling
of finely grated lemon zest.

SERVES 4

❊ In a large bowl, combine the lemon juice, wine, oil, garlic, oregano,
lemon zest, and salt and pepper. Stir in the chicken, eggplant, bell pepper, and onion. Cover and marinate in the refrigerator for 1 hour.

❊ Meanwhile, prepare an indirect-heat fire in a covered grill (see
page 13). Place 8 wooden skewers in water to cover and let stand for
at least 15 minutes.

❊ When the fire is hot, drain the skewers and thread the chicken, eggplant, bell pepper, and onion pieces onto them, alternating the pieces and
dividing them equally. Place on the perimeter of the grill rack directly
over the fire. Grill, turning the skewers once or twice, until the chicken
is browned, about 5 minutes total. Move the skewers to the center of the
grill rack so they are not directly over the fire. Cover the grill, open the
vents halfway, and cook, turning the skewers occasionally, until the
chicken is opaque throughout and the juices run clear and the vegetables are tender, 10–15 minutes longer.

❊ Transfer the skewers to a warmed platter or individual plates and
serve with the lemon wedges.

NUTRITIONAL ANALYSIS PER SERVING: Calories 281 (Kilojoules 1,180); Protein 41 g;
Carbohydrates 12 g; Total Fat 7 g; Saturated Fat 1 g; Cholesterol 99 mg; Sodium 120 mg;
Dietary Fiber 1 g

Chicken with Lemon, Garlic, and Parsley

PREP TIME: 15 MINUTES

COOKING TIME: 20 MINUTES

INGREDIENTS

2 tablespoons all-purpose (plain) flour

4 chicken breast halves, about ½ lb (250 g) each, skinned

3–5 cloves garlic

⅓ cup (½ oz/15 g) chopped fresh flat-leaf (Italian) parsley

1 tablespoon finely chopped lemon zest

2 tablespoons pure olive oil

salt and ground white or black pepper to taste

¾ cup (6 fl oz/180 ml) Chicken Stock *(page 15)*

½ cup (4 fl oz/125 ml) lemon juice

½ cup (4 fl oz/125 ml) Riesling, Chenin Blanc, or other fruity white wine

COOKING TIP: For an extra spark of aroma, taste, and color, substitute orange zest for half of the lemon zest.

Offer this refreshing dish on a hot summer's night. A garnish of lemon zest, parsley, and garlic recalls the *gremolata* that traditionally tops Milan's famed osso buco.

SERVES 4

❋ Spread the flour on a plate, then lightly coat both sides of each chicken breast with the flour, shaking off the excess. Finely chop 2 or 3 garlic cloves, then mince 1 or 2 additional cloves. Set aside the chopped garlic. In a small bowl, stir together the minced garlic, parsley, and lemon zest.

❋ In a frying pan over high heat, warm the olive oil. Add the chicken breasts and sauté, turning once, until lightly browned, about 2 minutes on each side. Transfer to a platter, season with salt and pepper, and set aside.

❋ Pour off all but 2 tablespoons of the fat from the pan. Add the finely chopped garlic to the pan and sauté over high heat until softened, about 20 seconds. Add the stock, lemon juice, and white wine, and deglaze the pan, stirring to remove any browned bits from the pan bottom. Bring to a boil and boil until slightly reduced, about 3 minutes.

❋ Return the chicken to the pan and reduce the heat to medium. Cook until the chicken is opaque throughout and the juices run clear, about 10 minutes. Using tongs, transfer to a warmed serving platter.

❋ Raise the heat to high and boil the pan sauce until reduced to about ¼ cup (2 fl oz/60 ml), about 5 minutes. Pour evenly over the chicken and sprinkle the parsley-garlic mixture evenly over the top.

NUTRITIONAL ANALYSIS PER SERVING: Calories 255 (Kilojoules 1,071); Protein 35 g; Carbohydrates 7 g; Total Fat 9 g; Saturated Fat 2 g; Cholesterol 86 mg; Sodium 121 mg; Dietary Fiber 0 g

Chicken with Mushroom Glaze

PREP TIME: 30 MINUTES

COOKING TIME: 25 MINUTES

INGREDIENTS

1 oz (30 g) dried porcini mushrooms

½ cup (4 fl oz/125 ml) boiling water

4 skinless, boneless chicken breast
halves, about 6 oz (185 g) each

3 tablespoons all-purpose (plain)
flour

2 tablespoons pure olive oil

1 shallot, minced

1 cup (3 oz/90 g) thinly sliced fresh
cremini mushrooms

1–2 tablespoons unsalted butter, at
room temperature

½ cup (4 fl oz/125 ml) Pinot Noir or
other medium-bodied red wine

½ cup (4 fl oz/125 ml) Chicken
Stock (*page 15*)

¼ cup (⅓ oz/10 g) snipped fresh
chives

COOKING TIP: For a more intense
mushroom flavor, use mushroom-
infused olive oil in place of the pure
olive oil.

Dried mushrooms give this quick sauté a deep and complex
flavor that belies its simple preparation. The addition of the
flour-and-butter paste, called a *beurre manié,* thickens the
sauce and imparts an appealing sheen to the finished dish.

SERVES 4

❀ Place the dried mushrooms in a small bowl and add the boiling
water. Let stand until softened, about 15 minutes. Drain, reserving the
soaking liquid. Pour the soaking liquid through a fine-mesh sieve lined
with a double thickness of cheesecloth (muslin) into a clean bowl. Finely
chop the mushrooms, and then set them and the soaking liquid aside.

❀ While the mushrooms are soaking, place each chicken breast between
2 sheets of plastic wrap and flatten with a meat pounder until an even
¼ inch (6 mm) thick. Spread 2 tablespoons of the flour on a plate, then
lightly coat both sides of each chicken piece with the flour, shaking off
the excess.

❀ In a frying pan over medium-high heat, warm the olive oil. Add the
chicken and sear, turning once, until browned, about 1½ minutes on each
side. Transfer to a plate and set aside.

❀ Reduce the heat to medium and add the shallot and fresh mushrooms to the pan. Sauté, adding 1 tablespoon of the butter if the mushrooms are sticking, until softened, about 4 minutes. Stir in the rehydrated
mushrooms, strained mushroom liquid, wine, and stock. Raise the heat
to medium-high and bring to a boil. Boil until reduced by half and the
red wine loses its bright color, 5–8 minutes.

❀ Meanwhile, in a small bowl, using your fingers, mix together 1 tablespoon butter and the remaining 1 tablespoon flour to form a paste. Drop
the paste into the sauce bit by bit, stirring to mix. Bring to a boil and
cook, stirring, until the sauce is thickened, about 5 minutes. Return the
chicken to the pan and cook until opaque throughout and the juices run
clear, about 5 minutes longer.

❀ Transfer the chicken to a warmed serving platter and spoon the sauce
over the top. Garnish with the chives and serve.

NUTRITIONAL ANALYSIS PER SERVING: Calories 321 (Kilojoules 1,348); Protein 37 g;
Carbohydrates 10 g; Total Fat 13 g; Saturated Fat 4 g; Cholesterol 98 mg; Sodium 110 mg;
Dietary Fiber 2 g

Chicken Curry

PREP TIME: 15 MINUTES

COOKING TIME: 40 MINUTES

INGREDIENTS

6–8 tablespoons (2¼–2½ oz/67–75 g)
all-purpose (plain) flour

4 chicken breast halves, about ½ lb
(250 g) each, skinned

4 chicken thighs, about 6 oz (185 g)
each, skinned

4 chicken drumsticks, about ¼ lb
(125 g) each, skinned

1 lb (500 g) chicken wings

2 tablespoons canola or safflower oil

2 yellow onions, chopped

2 cloves garlic, finely chopped

2–4 tablespoons curry powder or
⅓–½ cup (3–5 oz) curry paste

1½ cups (12 fl oz/375 ml) Chicken
Stock (page 15)

1½ cups (12 fl oz/375 ml) coconut
milk

salt and ground pepper to taste

FOR THE CONDIMENTS

1 cup (10 oz/315 g) mango chutney

¾ cup (4½ oz/140 g) diced tomato

½ cup (1½ oz/45 g) chopped green
(spring) onion

1 banana, peeled and thinly sliced

½ cup (3 oz/90 g) chopped peanuts
or cashews

½ cup (2 oz/60 g) unsweetened grated
coconut

The classic flavors of India come to the table in this simple chicken curry, which is served with an array of condiments. Accompany with steamed rice, which will absorb the delicious sauce. For a less rich, less caloric version of the curry, substitute an additional 1½ cups (12 fl oz/375 ml) stock for the coconut milk.

SERVES 6–8

❊ Spread the flour on a plate, then lightly coat both sides of each chicken piece with the flour, shaking off the excess.

❊ In a dutch oven or other large pot over high heat, warm the oil. Add the chicken pieces in batches and sauté, turning once, until browned, about 2 minutes on each side. Transfer to a plate and set aside.

❊ Reduce the heat to medium, add the onions to the pot, and sauté until softened, about 2 minutes. Stir in the garlic and curry powder or curry paste to taste, and sauté, stirring, for 1 minute longer. Raise the heat to high, stir in the stock, and deglaze the pot, stirring to remove any browned bits from the bottom.

❊ Return the chicken to the pot and bring to a boil. Add the coconut milk, reduce the heat to low, cover, and simmer until the chicken is opaque throughout, about 20 minutes. Season with salt and pepper.

❊ Transfer the chicken and sauce to a warmed serving bowl. Serve the condiments in small bowls for diners to add as desired.

NUTRITIONAL ANALYSIS PER SERVING: Calories 743 (Kilojoules 3,121); Protein 51 g; Carbohydrates 53 g; Total Fat 36 g; Saturated Fat 18 g; Cholesterol 149 mg; Sodium 607 mg; Dietary Fiber 4 g

Risotto with Smoked Chicken and Mushrooms

PREP TIME: 45 MINUTES

COOKING TIME: 40 MINUTES

INGREDIENTS

5 cups (40 fl oz/1.25 l) Chicken Stock (page 15)

2 tablespoons olive oil or unsalted butter

1 shallot, chopped

2 cloves garlic, minced

1 cup (3 oz/90 g) finely chopped fresh portobello, cremini, or porcini mushrooms

1½ cups (10½ oz/330 g) Arborio rice

2 plum (Roma) tomatoes, peeled, seeded, and chopped

2 teaspoons minced fresh thyme

2 teaspoons minced fresh rosemary

2 teaspoons minced fresh marjoram

½ cup (4 fl oz/125 ml) dry white wine

¼ lb (125 g) smoked chicken, julienned

salt and ground pepper to taste

¼ cup (½ oz/15 g) chopped fresh flat-leaf (Italian) parsley

COOKING TIP: Although Arborio is the most commonly available form of Italian rice used for risotto, you can also use varieties known as Carnaroli or Vialone Nano.

Use meat cut from smoked chicken breasts or thighs for the best flavor. The plump kernels of Italian Arborio rice contribute the creaminess that distinguishes the best risotto.

SERVES 4

❋ Pour the chicken stock into a saucepan and bring to a boil. Reduce the heat to maintain a gentle simmer.

❋ In a wide frying pan over medium heat, warm the oil or melt the butter. Add the shallot, garlic, and mushrooms and sauté until softened, about 3 minutes. Stir in the rice and cook, stirring, until the edges are translucent, about 2 minutes. Stir in the tomatoes, thyme, rosemary, and marjoram and sauté for 1 minute longer. Stir in the wine and bring to a boil.

❋ Add a ladleful of the simmering stock and continue to stir constantly over medium heat. When the liquid is almost fully absorbed, add another ladleful. Stir steadily to keep the rice from sticking, and continue to add more liquid, a ladleful at a time, as each previous ladleful is almost absorbed. The risotto is done when the rice is tender but firm, 25–30 minutes. Stir in the chicken and cook briefly to heat through. Season with salt and pepper.

❋ Transfer to a warmed serving dish or individual dishes and sprinkle with the parsley. Serve immediately.

NUTRITIONAL ANALYSIS PER SERVING: Calories 416 (Kilojoules 1,747); Protein 14 g; Carbohydrates 65 g; Total Fat 11 g; Saturated Fat 3 g; Cholesterol 21 mg; Sodium 236 mg; Dietary Fiber 2 g

Chicken Cacciatore

PREP TIME: 30 MINUTES

COOKING TIME: 45 MINUTES

INGREDIENTS

2 chicken breast halves, about ½ lb
(250 g) each, skinned

2 chicken thighs, about 6 oz (185 g)
each, skinned

2 chicken drumsticks, about ¼ lb
(125 g) each, skinned

2 chicken wings

1 tablespoon paprika

2 tablespoons olive oil

salt and ground pepper to taste

1 yellow onion, chopped

3 cloves garlic, minced

½ lb (250 g) fresh cremini mushrooms,
brushed clean and sliced

2 tablespoons all-purpose (plain)
flour

1 tablespoon chopped fresh marjoram

1 tablespoon chopped fresh basil

1 tablespoon chopped fresh thyme

1 cup (8 fl oz/250 ml) Chicken Stock
(page 15)

1 cup (8 fl oz/250 ml) Chianti or
other dry red wine

3 cups (18 oz/560 g) peeled, seeded,
and chopped tomatoes

Chicken cacciatore, or "hunter's style" chicken, is an old-fashioned Italian favorite. Fresh herbs, mushrooms, and tomatoes make this contemporary version particularly aromatic and hearty. Buttered pasta is a good accompaniment to enjoy with the chicken and its sauce.

SERVES 4

❊ Dust the chicken pieces with the paprika. In a heavy frying pan or dutch oven over high heat, warm the olive oil. Add the chicken in batches and cook, turning once, until browned, about 2 minutes on each side. Transfer to a plate and set aside. Season with salt and pepper.

❊ Pour off all but 2 tablespoons of the fat from the pan and place over medium heat. Add the onion and sauté until softened, about 2 minutes. Stir in the garlic and mushrooms and sauté until the mushrooms are softened, 1–2 minutes longer. Sprinkle the flour over the mushrooms and stir to incorporate and slightly cook the flour. Stir in the marjoram, basil, and thyme.

❊ Raise the heat to high, pour in the stock and wine, and deglaze the pan, stirring to remove any browned bits from the pan bottom. Add the tomatoes, stir well, and bring to a boil. Return the chicken to the pan and stir to combine with the sauce. Cover and reduce the heat to medium-low. Cook, stirring occasionally, until the chicken is opaque throughout, about 25 minutes.

❊ Using tongs, transfer the chicken pieces to a warmed platter. Spoon the sauce over the top and serve.

NUTRITIONAL ANALYSIS PER SERVING: Calories 352 (Kilojoules 1,478); Protein 42 g; Carbohydrates 19 g; Total Fat 12 g; Saturated Fat 3 g; Cholesterol 126 mg; Sodium 175 mg; Dietary Fiber 3 g

Chicken Tagine with Vegetables

PREP TIME: 20 MINUTES

COOKING TIME: 1½ HOURS

INGREDIENTS

2 tablespoons olive oil

2 chicken breast halves, about ½ lb (250 g) each, skinned

4 chicken thighs, about 6 oz (185 g) each, skinned

4 chicken drumsticks, about ¼ lb (125 g) each, skinned

salt to taste, plus ½ teaspoon

ground pepper to taste

1 green or red bell pepper (capsicum)

1 Asian (slender) eggplant (aubergine)

2 yellow onions

2 carrots

4 cloves garlic, finely chopped

1½ tablespoons powdered sumac

1 tablespoon sesame seeds

2 teaspoons minced fresh thyme

½ teaspoon ground cumin

3 cups (24 fl oz/750 ml) Chicken Stock (page 15)

⅓ cup (3 fl oz/80 ml) tomato paste

1½ cups (10½ oz/330 g) canned chickpeas (garbanzo beans)

1 tablespoon unsalted butter

1½ cups (7½ oz/235 g) instant couscous

1 tablespoon grated lemon zest mixed with ½ cup (¾ oz/20 g) chopped fresh parsley and 2 tablespoons chopped fresh mint

Named for the clay pot in which it is cooked, this tagine, or Moroccan stew, begins on the stove top in a frying pan and then goes into the oven in a clay baker or dutch oven. Powdered sumac, which is the ground dried berry of a bush of the same name, adds a fruity tartness to the dish. Za'tar, a North African seasoning, can be substituted for the sumac, sesame seeds, and thyme. Use about 2 tablespoons.

SERVES 4–6

❀ Preheat an oven to 350°F (180°C).

❀ In a frying pan over high heat, warm the oil. Add the chicken pieces in batches and sauté, turning once, until browned, about 2 minutes on each side. Transfer to a clay baker or a dutch oven. Season with salt and pepper.

❀ Seed and dice the bell pepper. Dice the eggplant and onions. Peel and dice the carrots. Add the bell pepper, eggplant, onions, and carrots to the same pan over medium heat and sauté until softened, about 5 minutes. Stir in the garlic, sumac, sesame seeds, thyme, and cumin and sauté until the garlic is softened, about 20 seconds. Add the stock and tomato paste, stir to mix well, and bring to a boil. Drain the chickpeas and add to the pan. Season with salt and pepper and pour over the chicken.

❀ Cover and bake for 40 minutes. Uncover, turn the chicken pieces, and continue to bake, uncovered, until the chicken is opaque throughout and the sauce has reduced slightly, about 15 minutes longer.

❀ Meanwhile, in a saucepan, bring 2¼ cups (18 fl oz/560 ml) water to a boil. Add the butter and the ½ teaspoon salt. When the butter melts, stir in the couscous and turn off the heat. Cover and let stand for 5 minutes. Just before serving, uncover and fluff the grains with a fork.

❀ Transfer the chicken and couscous to a warmed serving dish, sprinkle with the lemon zest mixture, and serve.

NUTRITIONAL ANALYSIS PER SERVING: Calories 611 (Kilojoules 2,566); Protein 52 g; Carbohydrates 61 g; Total Fat 17 g; Saturated Fat 4 g; Cholesterol 144 mg; Sodium 692 mg; Dietary Fiber 8 g

Chicken with Green and Black Olives

PREP TIME: 35 MINUTES

COOKING TIME: 45 MINUTES

INGREDIENTS

2 tablespoons pure olive oil

4 chicken thighs, about 6 oz (185 g) each, skinned

4 chicken drumsticks, about ¼ lb (125 g) each, skinned

1 shallot, finely chopped

½ cup (2½ oz/75 g) pitted and quartered Kalamata olives or other brine-cured Mediterranean-style black olives

8 pimiento-stuffed green olives, sliced

3 cloves garlic, minced

1 tablespoon drained capers

½ cup (4 fl oz/125 ml) Zinfandel, Cabernet Sauvignon, or other full-bodied red wine

½ cup (4 fl oz/125 ml) Chicken Stock (*page 15*)

salt and ground pepper to taste

3 tablespoons chopped fresh flat-leaf (Italian) parsley

The combination of capers, red wine, and both ripened and unripened olives imparts a piquancy to this Mediterranean-inspired dish.

SERVES 4

❀ In a large frying pan over high heat, warm the oil. Add the chicken pieces in batches and sauté, turning as needed, until browned on both sides, about 5 minutes total for each batch. Do not crowd the pan; as soon as the pieces are browned, transfer them to a plate and set aside.

❀ Reduce the heat to medium-high, add the shallot to the pan, and sauté until softened, about 2 minutes. Stir in the olives, garlic, capers, red wine, and stock. Bring to a boil and cook, stirring once or twice, until the flavors are blended and the red wine loses its bright color, about 10 minutes.

❀ Return the chicken to the pan, reduce the heat to medium-low, and cook until the chicken is opaque throughout and the juices run clear, about 15 minutes longer. Turn the chicken pieces occasionally to ensure even cooking. Uncover the pan during the last 5 minutes of cooking to reduce the sauce slightly. Season with salt and pepper.

❀ To serve, arrange the chicken pieces on a warmed serving platter, spoon the sauce over the top, and sprinkle with the parsley.

NUTRITIONAL ANALYSIS PER SERVING: Calories 325 (Kilojoules 1,365); Protein 33 g; Carbohydrates 5 g; Total Fat 19 g; Saturated Fat 3 g; Cholesterol 130 mg; Sodium 753 mg; Dietary Fiber 0 g

SERVING TIP: Fresh linguine or fettuccine, tossed with extra-virgin olive oil, makes a simple accompaniment for the chicken. If you like, spoon some of the sauce over the pasta.

Roast Chicken with Spinach-Rice Stuffing

PREP TIME: 40 MINUTES

COOKING TIME: 2 HOURS

INGREDIENTS

1 lb (500 g) spinach, tough stems removed

3 tablespoons water

2 tablespoons unsalted butter

1 yellow onion, chopped

1 cup (3 oz/90 g) sliced fresh cremini mushrooms

2 cloves garlic, chopped

2 teaspoons chopped fresh tarragon

2 teaspoons chopped fresh flat-leaf (Italian) parsley

2 teaspoons chopped fresh marjoram

2 cups (10 oz/315 g) cooked white rice

1 cup (8 oz/250 g) ricotta cheese

1 egg, beaten

salt and ground pepper to taste

⅓ cup (1½ oz/45 g) pine nuts, toasted

1 chicken, 3½–4 lb (1.75–2 kg)

FOR THE HERB PASTE

2 tablespoons olive oil

2 cloves garlic, minced

2 teaspoons paprika

2 teaspoons minced fresh tarragon

2 teaspoons minced fresh flat-leaf (Italian) parsley

salt and ground pepper to taste

The Italian-accented stuffing makes this roast chicken a suitable centerpiece for a special-occasion dinner.

SERVES 4–6

❋ Preheat an oven to 350°F (180°C). Place the spinach in a nonstick saucepan and add the water. Cover and cook over high heat, turning the leaves as needed, until wilted, about 3 minutes. Drain and let cool, then press out the excess liquid and chop.

❋ In a frying pan over medium heat, melt the butter. Add the onion and mushrooms and sauté until softened, about 3 minutes. Stir in the garlic and herbs and sauté for about 20 seconds longer. Add the spinach and cook, stirring, until the flavors are blended, about 2 minutes. Remove from the heat and let cool. In a bowl, combine the rice and ricotta and mix well. Stir in the spinach mixture, then mix in the egg. Season with salt and pepper. Stir in the pine nuts.

❋ Rinse the chicken and pat dry with paper towels. Stuff loosely with the rice mixture. Using kitchen string, tie the drumsticks together. Tuck the wing tips under the body. Butter a baking dish, put the remaining stuffing in it, and cover with aluminum foil.

❋ To make the herb paste, in a small bowl, combine the oil, garlic, paprika, tarragon, and parsley. Mix to form a paste and season with salt and pepper. Rub the entire outside of the chicken with the herb mixture. Place the chicken, breast side up, on a rack in a roasting pan. Roast until an instant-read thermometer inserted into the thickest part of the breast away from the bone registers 170°F (77°C) and in the thigh registers 185°F (85°C), or until the juices run clear when the thigh is pierced, about 1 hour and 40 minutes. Slip the extra stuffing into the oven during the last 20 minutes of cooking.

❋ Remove the chicken from the oven and transfer to a platter. Cover loosely with aluminum foil and let stand for 5–10 minutes. Remove the baking dish of stuffing and keep warm. Snip and remove the string. Spoon the stuffing from the cavity into the baking dish. Carve the chicken and serve with the stuffing.

NUTRITIONAL ANALYSIS PER SERVING: Calories 720 (Kilojoules 3,024); Protein 54 g; Carbohydrates 32 g; Total Fat 42 g; Saturated Fat 14 g; Cholesterol 212 mg; Sodium 231 mg; Dietary Fiber 4 g

Grilled Chicken Breasts with Tarragon Mustard

PREP TIME: 20 MINUTES, PLUS
1 HOUR FOR MARINATING

COOKING TIME: 25 MINUTES,
PLUS PREPARING FIRE

INGREDIENTS

⅓ cup (3 fl oz/80 ml) dry white wine

2–3 tablespoons tarragon-flavored
mustard

2 tablespoons extra-virgin olive oil

2 cloves garlic, minced

3 teaspoons finely chopped fresh
tarragon

1 teaspoon sugar

¼ teaspoon salt

¼ teaspoon ground pepper

2 whole chicken breasts, about 1 lb
(500 g) each, skinned

A tangy tarragon-mustard marinade complements this simple grilled chicken. Cooking the whole breast makes an attractive presentation for company. Carve the meat from the bone in thick slices so that each slice has a grill-marked edge.

SERVES 4

❈ In a small bowl, whisk together the wine, mustard, oil, garlic, 2 teaspoons of the tarragon, sugar, salt, and pepper. Scoop out and reserve ¼ cup (2 fl oz/60 ml) of the mustard mixture. Place the chicken in a nonaluminum dish. Pour the remaining mustard mixture evenly over the top, cover with plastic wrap, and refrigerate, turning the chicken occasionally, for at least 1 hour or for up to 4 hours.

❈ Prepare an indirect-heat fire in a covered grill (see page 13).

❈ About 20 minutes before the fire is ready, remove the chicken from the refrigerator and bring it to room temperature. When the fire is hot, place the chicken on the perimeter of the grill rack directly over the fire. Grill, turning once, until seared on both sides with grill marks, about 2 minutes on each side. Move the chicken pieces, skin side up, to the center of the grill rack so they are not directly over the fire. Cover the grill, open the vents halfway, and cook, turning once or twice and basting occasionally with the reserved marinade, until the chicken is opaque throughout and the juices run clear, about 20 minutes.

❈ Transfer to a warmed serving platter, carve into slices, and sprinkle with the remaining 1 teaspoon tarragon.

NUTRITIONAL ANALYSIS PER SERVING: Calories 220 (Kilojoules 924); Protein 34 g; Carbohydrates 1 g; Total Fat 7 g; Saturated Fat 1 g; Cholesterol 86 mg; Sodium 284 mg; Dietary Fiber 0 g

Fettuccine with Smoked Chicken and Goat Cheese

PREP TIME: 20 MINUTES

COOKING TIME: 20 MINUTES

INGREDIENTS

¼ cup (2 fl oz/60 ml) extra-virgin olive oil

1 small red (Spanish) onion, halved and sliced

½ red bell pepper (capsicum), seeded and sliced

10 slender asparagus stalks, tough ends removed and cut on the diagonal into 2-inch (5-cm) lengths

1 small zucchini (courgette), julienned

1 small yellow squash, julienned

¼ cup (2 fl oz/60 ml) water

½ cup (4 fl oz/125 ml) Chardonnay or other full-bodied white wine

2 cloves garlic, minced

¼ cup (2 oz/60 g) unsalted butter

3 oz (90 g) fresh goat cheese, cut into pieces

1 lb (500 g) fresh fettuccine or ¾ lb (375 g) dried fettuccine

3 plum (Roma) tomatoes, seeded and chopped

6 oz (185 g) smoked chicken, cut into thin strips

salt and ground pepper to taste

½ cup (¾ oz/20 g) chopped fresh basil

The natural sweetness of the vegetables contrasts nicely with the smokiness of the chicken and the tart goat cheese in this beautiful pasta dish.

SERVES 4–6

❀ In a large, nonstick frying pan over medium-high heat, warm the oil. Add the onion and bell pepper and sauté until just softened, 1–2 minutes. Stir in the asparagus, zucchini, and yellow squash, and add the water. Cover and cook, stirring occasionally, until all the vegetables are just tender and the water has evaporated, about 3 minutes. Remove from the heat.

❀ Meanwhile, in a small saucepan over high heat, combine the wine and garlic. Bring to a boil, reduce the heat to medium, and boil gently, stirring occasionally, until the wine is reduced by one-third, about 3 minutes. Add the butter and goat cheese and stir to melt. Remove from the heat.

❀ Bring a large saucepan three-fourths full of water to a boil over high heat. Add the pasta, stir well, and cook until al dente (tender but firm to the bite), about 2 minutes for the fresh pasta and 8–10 minutes for the dried pasta or according to the package directions. Drain and place in a warmed serving bowl.

❀ Just before the pasta is ready, add the tomatoes and chicken to the vegetables, then stir in the wine-garlic mixture. Season with salt and pepper and reheat to serving temperature.

❀ Pour the sauce over the pasta and toss well. Garnish with the basil and serve.

NUTRITIONAL ANALYSIS PER SERVING: Calories 581 (Kilojoules 2,440); Protein 22 g; Carbohydrates 57 g; Total Fat 29 g; Saturated Fat 11 g; Cholesterol 120 mg; Sodium 245 mg; Dietary Fiber 3 g

Chicken Pot Pie with Cornmeal Crust

PREP TIME: 50 MINUTES

COOKING TIME: 35 MINUTES

INGREDIENTS

2 tablespoons canola oil, plus ⅓ cup
(3 fl oz/80 ml)

6 green (spring) onions, chopped

1 green bell pepper (capsicum),
seeded and chopped

2 cloves garlic, minced

1½ lb (750 g) skinless, boneless
cooked chicken meat, cubed

1 can (3½ oz/105 g) chopped
Anaheim chiles, drained

1 serrano chile, seeded and minced

½ cup (½ oz/15 g) fresh cilantro
(fresh coriander) leaves

1 tablespoon chopped fresh oregano

½ teaspoon ground cumin

1 cup (5 oz/155 g) cooked white rice

½ cup (4 fl oz/125 ml) Chicken
Stock (page 15)

4 plum (Roma) tomatoes

salt to taste, plus ½ teaspoon

ground pepper to taste

1 cup (5 oz/155 g) each finely
ground yellow cornmeal and
all-purpose (plain) flour

1 tablespoon baking powder

1 teaspoon chili powder

½ cup (2 oz/60 g) Monterey jack
cheese, shredded

1 egg

1 cup (8 fl oz/250 ml) milk

Chicken pot pie, an American standard, borrows from the Mexican pantry with pleasantly spicy results in this delicious way to use leftover chicken. If you do not have already cooked chicken, poach 1½ lb (750 g) skinless, boneless chicken according to the directions on page 15. If you like, add 10 tomatillos, husks removed and the fruits coarsely chopped, to the chicken and rice before transferring to the baking dish.

SERVES 4–6

❀ Preheat an oven to 375°F (190°C).

❀ In a frying pan over medium-high heat, warm the 2 tablespoons oil. Add the green onions and bell pepper and sauté until softened, about 3 minutes. Add the garlic and sauté until softened, about 20 seconds longer. Remove from the heat and stir in the chicken, chiles, cilantro, oregano, cumin, rice, and stock. Seed and chop the tomatoes and add to the chicken and rice. Season with salt and pepper. Pour into a shallow, 6-cup (48–fl oz/1.5-l) baking dish.

❀ In a bowl, stir together the cornmeal, flour, baking powder, chili powder, and ½ teaspoon salt until well mixed. Stir in the jack cheese. In another bowl, using a whisk, beat the egg until blended. Then beat in the milk and the ⅓ cup (3 fl oz/80 ml) oil until well combined. Pour the liquid mixture into the flour mixture and stir to mix well. Spoon evenly over the chicken and rice.

❀ Bake until the crust is puffed and golden brown and the chicken filling is bubbling, 25–30 minutes. Serve hot directly from the dish.

NUTRITIONAL ANALYSIS PER SERVING: Calories 812 (Kilojoules 3,410); Protein 53 g; Carbohydrates 64 g; Total Fat 37 g; Saturated Fat 8 g; Cholesterol 183 mg; Sodium 1,184 mg; Dietary Fiber 4 g

Autumn Chicken Stew with Chanterelles

PREP TIME: 30 MINUTES

COOKING TIME: 1¼ HOURS

INGREDIENTS

1 pumpkin, 4–6 lb (2–3 kg)

4 chicken breast halves, about ½ lb (250 g) each, skinned

4 chicken thighs, about 6 oz (185 g) each, skinned

4 chicken drumsticks, about ¼ lb (125 g) each, skinned

1 lb (500 g) chicken wings

1 tablespoon paprika

2 tablespoons olive, canola, or other vegetable oil

salt and ground pepper to taste

½ lb (250 g) spicy Italian sausages

10–12 baby carrots, peeled

4 cloves garlic, slivered

1 yellow onion, chopped

1 red bell pepper (capsicum), seeded and chopped

2 tablespoons all-purpose (plain) flour

1½ cups (12 fl oz/375 ml) Chicken Stock (page 15)

1½ cups (12 fl oz/375 ml) Sauvignon Blanc or other white wine

8–12 small red potatoes

1–2 teaspoons each dried thyme and dried marjoram

½ lb (250 g) fresh chanterelle mushrooms, brushed clean and sliced

½ cup (¾ oz/20 g) chopped fresh flat-leaf (Italian) parsley

This hearty stew is thick with a variety of vegetables and spiked with hot Italian sausage.

SERVES 6–8

❈ Using a serrated knife, cut off the top 3–4 inches (7.5–10 cm) from the stem end of the pumpkin. Using a spoon, scrape out the seeds and fibers. Using a melon baller, scoop out the flesh and set aside.

❈ Dust the chicken pieces evenly with the paprika. In a dutch oven or other large pot over high heat, warm the oil. Add the chicken in batches and sauté, turning once, until browned, about 2 minutes on each side. Transfer to a plate, season with salt and pepper, and set aside. Reduce the heat to medium and add the sausages. Cook until browned on all sides, about 4 minutes total. Transfer to a cutting board and, when cool enough to handle, slice into rounds ½ inch (12 mm) thick.

❈ In the same pot over medium-high heat, add the carrots, garlic, onion, and bell pepper and sauté until softened, about 4 minutes. Stir in the flour and cook for 1 minute, stirring constantly. Raise the heat to high, pour in the stock, and deglaze the pot, stirring to remove any browned bits from the bottom. Then pour in the wine and add the reserved pumpkin, the potatoes, and thyme and marjoram to taste. Return the chicken and sausage to the pot, season with salt and pepper, and bring to a boil. Add half of the mushrooms. Reduce the heat to medium-low, cover partially, and simmer until the chicken is opaque throughout and the juices run clear and the potatoes are tender, about 20 minutes. Stir in the remaining mushrooms and cook until tender, 5–10 minutes longer.

❈ Transfer the stew to a tureen or other large serving dish. Sprinkle with the parsley and serve.

NUTRITIONAL ANALYSIS PER SERVING: Calories 656 (Kilojoules 2,755); Protein 55 g; Carbohydrates 43 g; Total Fat 29 g; Saturated Fat 8 g; Cholesterol 174 mg; Sodium 438 mg; Dietary Fiber 4 g

Baked Tomatoes and Zucchini

PREP TIME: 15 MINUTES

COOKING TIME: 1 HOUR

INGREDIENTS

2 tablespoons pure olive oil

1 red (Spanish) onion, sliced

salt and ground pepper to taste

¾ lb (375 g) plum (Roma) tomatoes, sliced

2 small zucchini (courgettes), about ¾ lb (375 g) total weight, sliced

1 tablespoon minced fresh basil

1 tablespoon minced fresh marjoram

¼ cup (2 fl oz/60 ml) water or Chicken Stock (page 15)

COOKING TIP: After the vegetables have baked, sprinkle with ¼ cup (1 oz/30 g) Parmesan cheese, slip them under a preheated broiler (griller), and broil (grill) until the top is golden brown.

Look for plum tomatoes and zucchini with similar diameters so that you have uniform slices to arrange attractively atop the sautéed red onions that form an aromatic base for this Mediterranean-inspired side dish.

SERVES 4–6

❊ Preheat an oven to 350°F (180°C). Butter or oil a shallow 2-qt (2-l) baking dish.

❊ In a frying pan over medium heat, warm the oil. Add the onion and sauté slowly until very soft and beginning to brown, about 10 minutes. Transfer the onion slices to the prepared baking dish, spreading them evenly over the bottom. Season with salt and pepper.

❊ Arrange the tomato slices and zucchini slices over the onion in alternate rows. Sprinkle with the basil and marjoram and season with salt and pepper. Pour the water or stock evenly over the vegetables.

❊ Cover and bake until the vegetables are bubbling and tender, about 40 minutes. Remove from the oven, uncover, and serve hot directly from the dish.

NUTRITIONAL ANALYSIS PER SERVING: Calories 108 (Kilojoules 454); Protein 3 g; Carbohydrates 12 g; Total Fat 7 g; Saturated Fat 1 g; Cholesterol 2 mg; Sodium 27 mg; Dietary Fiber 2 g

Garlic Mashed Potatoes

PREP TIME: 15 MINUTES

COOKING TIME: 40 MINUTES

INGREDIENTS

6 cloves garlic, unpeeled

2 tablespoons olive oil

1 tablespoon finely chopped fresh rosemary or thyme

3 baking potatoes, about 1½ lb (750 g) total weight, peeled or unpeeled, cut into 2-inch (5-cm) chunks

¼ cup (2 oz/60 g) unsalted butter

½ cup (4 fl oz/125 ml) milk

salt and ground white or black pepper to taste

¼ cup (¾ oz/20 g) snipped fresh chives (optional)

COOKING TIP: Many potato varieties are appropriate for this side dish. Mashing baking potatoes yields fluffy results. For a smoother, creamier texture, use white or red new potatoes or Yukon Gold potatoes.

Roasting garlic in the oven mellows its flavor and brings out its natural sweetness. Adding it to mashed potatoes seasoned with fresh herbs elevates an old-fashioned favorite.

SERVES 4–6

❀ Preheat an oven to 325°F (165°C).

❀ Place the garlic cloves in a small baking dish. Drizzle with the olive oil and sprinkle with the rosemary or thyme. Cover with aluminum foil and bake until very soft, 35–40 minutes. Remove from the oven and, when cool enough to handle, squeeze the garlic from the sheaths into a small bowl. Mash with a fork. Strain the oil through a fine-mesh sieve held over the garlic and mix well.

❀ Meanwhile, place the potatoes in a saucepan and add water to cover by 1 inch (2.5 cm). Bring to a boil and cook, uncovered, until tender, about 20 minutes.

❀ Just before the potatoes are ready, in a small saucepan, combine the butter and milk over low heat, and heat until the butter is melted and the mixture is hot. Drain the potatoes, transfer to a warmed bowl, and mash well with a fork or potato masher. Alternatively, push them through a food mill or ricer placed over a warmed bowl.

❀ Add the butter-milk mixture to the potatoes and stir until smooth. Mix in the garlic and season with salt and pepper. Stir in the chives, if using, and serve immediately.

NUTRITIONAL ANALYSIS PER SERVING: Calories 257 (Kilojoules 1,079); Protein 3 g; Carbohydrates 27 g; Total Fat 16 g; Saturated Fat 7 g; Cholesterol 28 mg; Sodium 19 mg; Dietary Fiber 2 g

Chard, Spinach, and Mushroom Gratin

PREP TIME: 25 MINUTES

COOKING TIME: 35 MINUTES

INGREDIENTS

4 tablespoons (2 oz/60 g) unsalted butter

1 shallot, minced

6 oz (185 g) fresh cremini mushrooms, brushed clean and sliced, or portobello mushrooms, brushed clean and chopped

1½ teaspoons dry mustard

½ cup (4 fl oz/125 ml) water

2 tablespoons red wine vinegar

1 small bunch red or green Swiss chard, about 6 oz (185 g), trimmed and coarsely chopped

1 bunch spinach, about ¾ lb (375 g), tough stems removed and coarsely chopped

salt and ground pepper to taste

⅓ cup (1½ oz/45 g) fine dried bread crumbs

3–4 tablespoons grated Parmesan cheese

1 tablespoon olive oil

The topping of bread crumbs and Parmesan cheese turns a rich golden brown in the oven, complementing the earthy flavors of the greens and mushrooms.

SERVES 4–6

❊ Preheat an oven to 325°F (165°C). Butter a shallow 1-qt (1-l) baking dish.

❊ In a large nonstick frying pan over medium heat, melt 2 tablespoons of the butter. Add the shallot and mushrooms and sauté until softened, about 2 minutes. Stir in the mustard and sauté for 10 seconds longer. Stir in the water and vinegar. Add the chard and spinach, a handful at a time, waiting for each handful to wilt before adding the next one. It should take about 30 seconds for each addition to wilt. When all of the greens have been added, season with salt and pepper and remove from the heat.

❊ Transfer to the prepared baking dish. Sprinkle the bread crumbs and cheese evenly over the top and then drizzle evenly with the oil. Dot with the remaining 2 tablespoons butter.

❊ Bake until heated through and the top is golden brown, 15–20 minutes. Remove from the oven and serve directly from the dish.

NUTRITIONAL ANALYSIS PER SERVING: Calories 191 (Kilojoules 802); Protein 5 g; Carbohydrates 11 g; Total Fat 15 g; Saturated Fat 7 g; Cholesterol 30 mg; Sodium 247 mg; Dietary Fiber 3 g

Ginger-Glazed Vegetables

PREP TIME: 20 MINUTES

COOKING TIME: 15 MINUTES

INGREDIENTS

2 tablespoons safflower oil

1 zucchini (courgette), julienned

1 large red bell pepper (capsicum),
seeded and julienned

1 daikon, about ¼ lb (125 g), peeled
and julienned

1 tablespoon peeled and chopped
fresh ginger

2 cloves garlic, minced

1 teaspoon sugar

½ cup (4 fl oz/125 ml) water

salt and ground black or white pepper

¼ cup (⅓ oz/10 g) chopped fresh
flat-leaf (Italian) parsley (optional)

COOKING TIP: In the spring, substitute 1 lb (500 g) asparagus, cut
into 2-inch (5-cm) lengths, for the
zucchini, bell pepper, and daikon.
In the fall, use 1¼ cups (6 oz/185 g)
cubed eggplant (aubergine) and
1¼ cups (4½ oz/140 g) quartered
fresh mushrooms.

Julienne strips of zucchini, red bell pepper, and daikon quickly
sautéed and aromatic with ginger make a light accompaniment
for roast chicken or an Asian-inspired main course. Daikon, a
large Asian radish with crisp white flesh, can be found in Asian
markets and well-stocked food stores.

SERVES 4–6

❀ In a frying pan over medium-high heat, warm the oil. Add the zucchini,
bell pepper, daikon, ginger, garlic, and sugar and sauté until the vegetables
are wilted, 1–2 minutes. Add the water and cook until the vegetables are
tender, about 5 minutes.

❀ Raise the heat to high and boil until the liquid evaporates and the
sugar and the other ingredients have caramelized to a shiny glaze, about
4 minutes. Season with salt and pepper.

❀ Transfer to a warmed serving bowl. Garnish with the parsley, if desired,
and serve immediately.

NUTRITIONAL ANALYSIS PER SERVING: Calories 68 (Kilojoules 286); Protein 1 g;
Carbohydrates 5 g; Total Fat 6 g; Saturated Fat 1 g; Cholesterol 0 mg; Sodium 6 mg;
Dietary Fiber 0 g

Perfect Pilaf

PREP TIME: 15 MINUTES

COOKING TIME: 35 MINUTES

INGREDIENTS

1½ cups (10½ oz/330 g) long-grain white rice

2 tablespoons unsalted butter or canola oil

½ cup (2 oz/60 g) chopped yellow onion or 1 shallot, chopped

3 cups (24 fl oz/750 ml) Chicken Stock *(page 15)* or water, heated

salt and ground black or white pepper

1 tablespoon chopped fresh flat-leaf (Italian) parsley and /or snipped chives (optional)

COOKING TIP: To turn the pilaf into a main dish, break up 1 oz (30 g) dried spaghetti or vermicelli into 1-inch (2.5-cm) lengths and add to the frying pan along with the rice. Add 1 cup (6 oz/185 g) cooked cubed chicken meat with the liquid.

This basic rice side dish can be embellished with vegetables, such as 1 cup (3 oz/90 g) sautéed sliced mushrooms, 1 cup (5 oz/155 g) sautéed diced bell peppers (capsicums), or 1 cup (6 oz/185 g) chopped, seeded tomatoes.

SERVES 4–6

❂ Preheat an oven to 350°F (180°C). Butter a shallow 2-qt (2-l) baking dish.

❂ Rinse the rice, changing the water until it runs clear. Set aside.

❂ In a frying pan over medium heat, melt the butter or heat the oil. Add the onion or shallot and sauté until softened, about 2 minutes. Stir in the rice and sauté until the grains become translucent at the edges, 1–2 minutes. Transfer to the prepared baking dish, add the hot stock or water, season with salt and pepper, and stir to mix.

❂ Cover and bake until all the liquid is absorbed, 25–30 minutes. Remove from the oven, uncover, and fluff with a fork. Garnish with the parsley and/or chives (if desired) and serve immediately.

NUTRITIONAL ANALYSIS PER SERVING: Calories 285 (Kilojoules 1,197); Protein 6 g; Carbohydrates 50 g; Total Fat 6 g; Saturated Fat 4 g; Cholesterol 16 mg; Sodium 54 mg; Dietary Fiber 1 g

Almond-Fruit Tart

PREP TIME: 50 MINUTES

COOKING TIME: 30 MINUTES

INGREDIENTS

FOR THE CRUST

1 heaping cup (6 oz/185 g) almonds

2 tablespoons sugar

1¼ cups (6½ oz/200 g) all-purpose (plain) flour

¾ cup (6 oz/185 g) chilled unsalted butter, cut into pieces

2–3 tablespoons almond liqueur or corn syrup

¼ lb (125 g) almond paste

2 tablespoons unsalted butter, at room temperature

1 egg white

1 pt (8 oz/250 g) blueberries, or 4 or 5 small peaches, pitted and sliced

1 tablespoon water

1 tablespoon (1 envelope) unflavored gelatin

¾ cup (7½ oz/235 g) red currant jelly or apple jelly

A beautiful nut crust is the perfect palette for berries or sliced stone fruits. Whole raspberries or blackberries, or sliced strawberries, can be used in place of the blueberries, and nectarines can stand in for the peaches.

MAKES ONE 9-INCH (23-CM) TART; SERVES 6–8

❋ Preheat an oven to 350°F (180°C).

❋ To make the crust, in a food processor, combine the almonds and sugar and process until fairly finely ground. Add the flour and pulse to mix. Add the butter and pulse until the mixture resembles coarse meal. Add 2 tablespoons of the almond liqueur or corn syrup and pulse to bring the dough together in a rough mass, adding the remaining 1 tablespoon liqueur or syrup if the mixture is too dry.

❋ Transfer the mixture to a 9-inch (23-cm) tart pan with a removable bottom. Using your fingers, pat it evenly over the bottom and up the sides of the pan. Bake until light brown and set, about 25 minutes.

❋ Meanwhile, in a bowl, combine the almond paste and butter and beat with an electric mixer until smooth. Beat in the egg white.

❋ When the crust is ready, remove from the oven and let cool for about 5 minutes. Spread the almond paste mixture evenly over the bottom of the warm crust. Let cool completely, then arrange the berries or peaches decoratively over the top.

❋ Place the water in a small bowl, sprinkle the gelatin over the top, stir, and let stand for several minutes to soften. In a small saucepan over low heat, warm the jelly until it melts, about 5 minutes. Stir in the dissolved gelatin until melted, about 30 seconds. Remove from the heat and let cool slightly. Brush the jelly glaze evenly over the fruit. Let cool completely and serve at room temperature.

NUTRITIONAL ANALYSIS PER SERVING: Calories 632 (Kilojoules 2,654); Protein 11 g; Carbohydrates 61 g; Total Fat 40 g; Saturated Fat 16 g; Cholesterol 62 mg; Sodium 29 mg; Dietary Fiber 4 g

Ginger Cookies

PREP TIME: 20 MINUTES, PLUS
CHILLING OVERNIGHT

COOKING TIME: 20 MINUTES

INGREDIENTS

½ cup (4 oz/125 g) unsalted butter,
at room temperature

1 cup (7 oz/220 g) firmly packed
brown sugar or 1 cup (8 oz/250 g)
granulated sugar

1 egg

1¾ cups (9 oz/280 g) all-purpose
(plain) flour

½ teaspoon baking soda (bicarbon-
ate of soda)

¼ teaspoon salt

½ cup (1½ oz/45 g) finely chopped
crystallized ginger

½ teaspoon vanilla extract (essence)

STORAGE TIP: If not serving the
cookies immediately after baking,
transfer to an airtight container and
store for up to 1 week.

Tiny chunks of crystallized ginger dot these not-too-sweet
cookies. You will need to start making them a day in advance
of serving. Be sure not to overbake them or they will become
hard and brittle.

MAKES ABOUT 30 COOKIES

❋ In a bowl, using an electric mixer, beat together the butter and sugar
until light and fluffy, about 4 minutes. Beat in the egg. In another bowl,
stir together the flour, baking soda, and salt. Beat the flour mixture into
the butter mixture. Using a spoon or spatula, stir in the ginger and
vanilla. Divide the dough in half.

❋ On a lightly floured work surface, roll each half into a log about
1½ inches (4 cm) in diameter. Wrap the logs separately in plastic wrap,
place on a baking sheet, and refrigerate overnight.

❋ Preheat an oven to 325°F (165°C). Lightly grease 2 baking sheets or
line the bottoms with parchment (baking) paper or waxed paper.

❋ Unwrap the logs and, using a sharp knife, cut each log into slices
½ inch (12 mm) thick. Place on the prepared baking sheets, spacing
them about 1 inch (2.5 cm) apart.

❋ Bake, one sheet at a time, until the cookies are lightly browned
around the edges, 8–10 minutes. Remove from the oven and transfer
the cookies to racks. Let cool completely and serve.

NUTRITIONAL ANALYSIS PER COOKIE: Calories 94 (Kilojoules 395); Protein 1 g;
Carbohydrates 14 g; Total Fat 4 g; Saturated Fat 2 g; Cholesterol 15 mg; Sodium 45 mg;
Dietary Fiber 0 g

Tropical Fruit in Citrus Syrup

PREP TIME: 25 MINUTES

COOKING TIME: 10 MINUTES

INGREDIENTS

½ cup (5 oz/155 g) red currant jelly
or apple jelly

¼ cup (2 fl oz/60 ml) water or
orange juice

1 tablespoon sugar

1 teaspoon grated lemon or orange
zest

⅛ teaspoon vanilla extract (essence)

½ cup (2 oz/60 g) unsweetened
shredded coconut or ½ cup (2 oz/
60 g) whole almonds

2 cups (12 oz/375 g) cubed pineapple

1 mango, pitted, peeled, and cubed

1 papaya, seeded, peeled, and cubed

1 banana, peeled and cubed

SERVING TIP: Beat ½ cup (4 fl oz/
125 ml) heavy (double) cream with
2 tablespoons confectioners' (icing)
sugar and ½ teaspoon vanilla extract
(essence) until stiff, and top each
serving with a spoonful of the sweetened cream.

Fresh fruits are coated in a light syrup and then topped with coconut or toasted nuts. You can use the combination here or create your own complementary mix from the tropical fruits available in the market.

SERVES 6–8

❁ In a saucepan over high heat, combine the jelly, water or orange juice, sugar, lemon or orange zest, and vanilla. Bring to a boil, stirring to dissolve the sugar, and cook until the jelly has melted and the ingredients are well blended, 2–3 minutes. Remove from the heat and let cool.

❁ If using almonds, preheat an oven to 350°F (180°C). Spread the almonds on a baking sheet and toast until lightly toasted and fragrant, 5–7 minutes. Remove from the oven, let cool, and chop. Set aside.

❁ Place the fruits in a large serving bowl or in individual serving dishes. Pour the cooled syrup evenly over the fruit and stir to mix. Top with the coconut or almonds and serve.

NUTRITIONAL ANALYSIS PER SERVING: Calories 191 (Kilojoules 802); Protein 1 g; Carbohydrates 37 g; Total Fat 6 g; Saturated Fat 5 g; Cholesterol 0 mg; Sodium 13 mg; Dietary Fiber 2 g

Rum-Raisin Bread Pudding

PREP TIME: 30 MINUTES

COOKING TIME: 1 HOUR

INGREDIENTS

½ cup (3 oz/90 g) golden raisins (sultanas)

¼ cup (2 fl oz/60 ml) rum or brandy

4 cups (8 oz/250 g) day-old bread cubes

½ cup (4 oz/125 g) sugar

⅓ cup (3 oz/90 g) unsalted butter, melted and cooled

3 eggs, beaten

1½ cups (12 fl oz/375 ml) milk

1½ teaspoons vanilla extract (essence)

½ teaspoon lemon extract (essence)

½ teaspoon ground cinnamon

1 tart apple, cored and cubed

COOKING TIP: Dried cherries or cranberries can be used in place of the raisins.

Raisins plumped in rum contribute the signature flavor to this custardy pudding. If you like, sprinkle each serving with granulated or confectioners' (icing) sugar.

SERVES 4–6

❈ In a small bowl, combine the raisins and rum or brandy and let stand for 30 minutes.

❈ While the raisins are soaking, preheat an oven to 325°F (165°C). Butter an 8-inch (20-cm) square baking dish or 4–6 custard cups.

❈ Spread the bread cubes on a baking sheet and bake until lightly toasted, about 10 minutes. Remove from the oven and set aside.

❈ In a large bowl, beat together the sugar, butter, eggs, milk, vanilla and lemon extracts, and cinnamon until well blended. Stir in the bread cubes, apple, and raisins and rum. Let stand until the bread cubes soak up most of the liquid, about 5 minutes. Stir again and pour into the baking dish or divide among the custard cups.

❈ Bake until a knife inserted into the center comes out clean, 30–40 minutes for custard cups, 50–60 minutes for a baking dish. Remove from the oven and serve hot or at room temperature.

NUTRITIONAL ANALYSIS PER SERVING: Calories 502 (Kilojoules 2,108); Protein 11 g; Carbohydrates 67 g; Total Fat 22 g; Saturated Fat 12 g; Cholesterol 178 mg; Sodium 322 mg; Dietary Fiber 3 g

Tarte Tatin

PREP TIME: 40 MINUTES, PLUS
10 MINUTES FOR FREEZING

COOKING TIME: 1 HOUR

INGREDIENTS

FOR THE PASTRY

1 cup (5 oz/155 g) all-purpose
(plain) flour

2 tablespoons sugar

pinch of salt

¼ cup (2 oz/60 g) chilled unsalted
butter, cut into pieces

2–3 tablespoons water

FOR THE FILLING

¼ cup (2 oz/60 g) unsalted butter

¾ cup (6 oz/185 g) sugar

1 teaspoon finely grated lemon zest

½ teaspoon ground cinnamon

¼ teaspoon ground nutmeg

4 large tart apples, about 2 lb (1 kg)
total weight, peeled, cored, and
cut into wedges

SERVING TIP: Accompany each wedge
of tart with a scoop of vanilla ice
cream or a dollop of lightly sweetened whipped cream.

Lemon, cinnamon, and nutmeg scent this French classic first made by the Tatin sisters of the Loire Valley. A cast-iron frying pan is ideal for preparing this upside-down tart; a nonstick frying pan makes unmolding the tart all the easier.

SERVES 4–6

❀ Preheat an oven to 375°F (190°C).

❀ To make the pastry, in a bowl, stir together the flour, sugar, and salt. Using a pastry blender or your fingers, work in the butter until the mixture resembles coarse meal. Using a fork, stir in the water, a little at a time, until the mixture comes together.

❀ Transfer the dough to a lightly floured work surface. Roll out into a round 9 inches (23 cm) in diameter and ¼ inch (6 mm) thick. Carefully transfer to a sheet of plastic wrap or waxed paper, cover with a second sheet, and refrigerate for 1 hour or freeze for 10 minutes.

❀ To make the filling, place a heavy, ovenproof 9-inch (23-cm) frying pan over medium-high heat. Add the butter and, when it melts, stir in the sugar. Cook, stirring continuously, until the sugar begins to caramelize, about 10 minutes. As the sugar begins to turn golden, stir in the lemon zest, cinnamon, and nutmeg. Arrange the apple wedges in the pan in a single layer. When they begin to take on a brown color and are almost tender, after about 5 minutes longer, place in the oven.

❀ Bake for 10 minutes. Remove from the oven and carefully lay the chilled pastry round over the apples, tucking the edges of the pastry around the apples. Return to the oven and bake until the crust is browned and the apples are bubbling, 15–20 minutes. If the pastry doesn't brown in that time, turn on the broiler (griller) and broil (grill) until browned, about 2 minutes.

❀ Let cool for 15 minutes. To unmold, place a platter on top of the frying pan and invert the pan and platter together. Lift off the pan and tuck any loose apple wedges in place. Cut into wedges and serve warm or at room temperature.

NUTRITIONAL ANALYSIS PER SERVING: Calories 506 (Kilojoules 2,125); Protein 3 g; Carbohydrates 84 g; Total Fat 19 g; Saturated Fat 12 g; Cholesterol 49 mg; Sodium 30 mg; Dietary Fiber 4 g

GLOSSARY

AVOCADOS

Appreciated for thousands of years in Central America, these vegetable-fruits were carried to North America and Europe by Spanish explorers and are grown today around the world. As a result, avocados are available year-round. Among the most widely cultivated of the hundreds of varieties is the **Haas** avocado (below), which comes into season in spring and summer, when its buttery-smooth, cool green flesh is most welcome. The Haas is

easily distinguished by its pearlike shape and very pebbly, dark greenish black skin. Both characteristics contributed to the quaint name

by which it was long known: alligator pear.

To assess the ripeness of an avocado, squeeze it in your palm; it should yield to gentle pressure. To remove the pit neatly, use a sharp knife to cut down to the pit lengthwise all around the avocado. Gently twist the halves in opposite directions to separate. Cup the half with the pit in the palm of one hand, with your fingers safely clear. Holding a sturdy, sharp knife with the other hand, carefully strike the pit with the blade of the knife, wedging the blade firmly into the pit. Then twist and lift the knife to remove the pit.

BELL PEPPERS

These sweet-fleshed, bell-shaped peppers, also known as capsicums, have long been pantry staples featured in sautéed, stewed, and baked chicken dishes, as well as in such specialties as fajitas, lasagne, and tagines. They are most commonly found in their unripened, sharp-tasting green form, but

ripened red or golden yellow varieties are sold in markets with increasing frequency. The latter add a sweeter flavor and bright color to many chicken dishes and other recipes.

BREAD CRUMBS

Fine dried bread crumbs are used to give a crisp coating to fried chicken and to add body to ground (minced) chicken.

To make bread crumbs, trim away the crusts from ½ pound (250 g) fresh coarse country white bread. Put the bread in a food processor and process to make soft fresh crumbs. Spread them on a baking sheet and bake in a preheated 325°F (165°C) oven until dry, about 15 minutes. Let the crumbs cool, then process again until fine; return to the oven to bake until lightly colored, stirring once or twice, about 15 minutes.

CHICKEN, SMOKED

Sold in specialty-food stores and delicatessens, smoked chicken has a sweet, mildly smoky flavor and tender texture that emphasize the natural qualities of the bird.

EQUIPMENT

FRYING PAN
An essential piece of equipment for fried and sautéed chicken dishes, a good frying pan is made of heavy stainless steel, thick aluminum, cast iron, or heavy enamel, all of which hold and transfer heat well for rapid browning. Choose a frying pan of substantial width and depth so that chicken pieces can be turned easily and can cook without crowding and with minimum spattering.

KETTLE GRILL
Available in a range of sizes, this fuel-efficient grill is distinguished by its deep, hemispherical fire pan and domed cover, both of which are vented to allow ease of temperature control for quick direct-heat and slower indirect-heat cooking.

V-SHAPED ROASTING RACK
Made of thick stainless-steel rods, this rack is sturdy enough to hold a large chicken, a turkey, or other large roast inside a roasting pan. By raising the chicken off the bottom of the pan, the rack ensures air circulation for even cooking and allows access to pan juices for basting. The handles facilitate removing the bird from the roasting pan.

CHILES

Ranging from mildly spicy to fiery hot, chile peppers spark up the mild taste of chicken. Many food stores now carry a wide range of chiles. Also look for chiles in Latin American, Asian, or farmers' markets. Whatever kinds of chiles you use, always bear in mind that their heat comes from volatile oils that can also cause a painful burning sensation in your eyes, cuts on your hands, or other sensitive areas. After handling the peppers, wash your hands thoroughly with warm, soapy water; alternatively, wear kitchen gloves.

ANAHEIM

Large, slender green chile about 6 inches (15 cm) long and 2 inches (5 cm) wide. Mild to slightly hot, it is also sometimes called long green or California chile and is similar to, but somewhat milder than, the New Mexican chile. Roasted and peeled Anaheims are widely available canned, most often under the Ortega label.

CHILE PASTE

This popular Asian seasoning and condiment, sold in jars in well-stocked food stores and in Asian markets, is made by crushing hot red chiles with salt, usually vinegar, and often garlic. Just a touch of the paste adds a rich, fiery taste.

CHILI POWDER

Commercial blend of spices featuring ground dried chiles along with such other seasonings as cumin, oregano, cloves, coriander, pepper, and salt. Best purchased in small quantities because the flavor diminishes rapidly after opening.

JALAPEÑO

Fiery chile (below, top) distinguished by its thick flesh and small, tapered body measuring 2–3 inches (5–7.5 cm) long and up to 1½ inches (4 cm) wide at the stem end. Named after the capital of the Mexican state of Veracruz, jalapeños are usually sold green and less frequently red, and may also be purchased pickled in brine. Dried, smoked jalapeños, called chipotle chiles, are commonly canned in a thick, vinegar-based adobo sauce.

SERRANO

Used fresh in both its underripe green and its ripened red forms, this chile (above, bottom) is as hot as a jalapeño, but has a distinctly sharper taste. Serranos generally measure no more than 2 inches (5 cm) long and ½ inch (12 mm) wide.

THAI

Small, thin, fiery red or green chiles similar in looks and heat to serranos, which may be substituted.

COCONUT MILK

Not to be confused with the watery liquid found inside whole coconuts or the sweetened coconut cream sold as a bar mixer, coconut milk is extracted from coconut flesh by puréeing it with hot water and then straining it. Coconut milk, available canned, is used as a flavorful base for Indian curries and Southeast Asian dishes featuring chicken. Before use, shake well to reincorporate the thick layer of cream that rises to the top. To reduce the fat in dishes calling for coconut milk, do not shake the can; instead, spoon off the cream and use the lighter liquid beneath it.

EGGPLANT, ASIAN

Appreciated for its rich taste and texture, this vegetable-fruit comes in many shapes, sizes, and colors, but is most familiar for its deep purple skin. In Asian kitchens, smaller, elongated, slender types, often labeled Asian eggplants, are used. These tend to have a milder flavor and fewer seeds than larger globe-shaped varieties.

GARLIC

Prized for its pungent and highly aromatic taste, garlic is an indispensable ingredient in many chicken dishes. For the best flavor, buy whole heads of garlic, separating individual cloves from the head as you need them. Do not buy more than you will use in 1–2 weeks.

GINGER, FRESH

Although it resembles a root, this sweet-hot Asian seasoning is actually the underground stem, or rhizome, of the tropical ginger plant.

HERBS

The flavor of chicken is complemented by a wide range of both fresh and dried herbs. To store fresh herbs, refrigerate them, either with their stem ends in a glass of water or wrapped in damp paper towels inside a plastic bag.

Spicy-sweet, tender-leafed **basil** goes especially well in chicken dishes that also feature tomatoes. **Bay leaves** (below), the dried whole leaves of the bay laurel tree, have a pungent, spicy flavor that is favored in long-simmered dishes; seek out the French variety, which has a milder, sweeter flavor than bay leaves from California. **Chervil** is a delicate springtime herb whose small leaves resemble flat-leaf (Italian) parsley and taste like a cross between parsley and anise, making them a welcome addition to chicken salads. **Cilantro** (below),

also called fresh coriander or Chinese parsley, is a leafy herb that looks like flat-leaf parsley and has a highly aromatic, astringent taste that complements spicy dishes from India, Southeast Asia, and Mexico. Fresh or dried, pungent **marjoram** and its stronger-flavored cousin, **oregano**, go well with chicken dishes that include tomatoes. Distinctively sweet **tarragon** (at right), whether fresh or dried, recalls the flavor and fragrance of anise and is a popular addition to chicken dishes. **Thyme** (below), a brightly

flavored herb native to the eastern Mediterranean, also goes well in a wide array of chicken dishes.

MUSTARD

Derived from the seeds of the mustard plant, this popular, pungent spice complements chicken dishes in many forms. **Dry mustard** is an intensely hot powder ground from the seeds. **Dijon mustard**, made in the French city of Dijon from dark brown mustard seeds (unless otherwise marked blanc) and white wine or wine vinegar, has a distinctive pale color and moderately hot, sharp flavor. Other forms of prepared mustard gain unique character from their own particular additions. **Prepared yellow mustard**, for example, is the most widespread American variety; its extra pungency comes from the ground turmeric that also bolsters its vivid yellow hue. Many mustard preparations incorporate complementary herbs as well, with tarragon among the most popular.

MUSHROOMS

The mild taste and smooth texture of chicken make it the perfect foil for the earthy flavor and satisfying chewiness of many different types of mushroom. A wide variety of mushrooms may be found in well-stocked food stores, greengrocers, and farmers' markets.

CHANTERELLE

Wild mushrooms now also cultivated commercially, these pale yellow, trumpet-shaped specimens are distinguished by their subtle flavor.

CREMINI

Resembling common cultivated mushrooms in their shape and size, this variety has a rich flavor complemented by a medium brown skin and deep ivory flesh.

DRIED CHINESE BLACK

This is the dried form of a mushroom widely known today by its Japanese name, *shiitake*. Reconstituted in liquid before use, these meaty mushrooms contribute a robust taste and texture to recipes.

OYSTER

So named for its pale grayish pink color, shellfishlike shape, and faint resemblance in taste to oysters, this tender Asian variety may be found in Asian markets, well-stocked food stores, and farmers' markets.

PORCINI

The Italian name for these wild brown-capped mushrooms means "little pigs"—an apt description for their plump forms. Prized for their tender texture and rich flavor, porcini are found fresh in summer and autumn. During the rest of the year, dried porcini are widely sold in Italian delicatessens and specialty-food stores. They are also known by the French as *cèpes*.

PORTOBELLO

The flat, circular brown caps of these mushrooms, the fully matured form of cremini, grow as large as about 4 inches (10 cm) in diameter. They are enjoyed for their rich taste and texture when cooked.

OILS

Many different kinds of cooking oil may be used in chicken dishes, depending on the desired effect. Flavorless vegetable and seed oils such as **canola, safflower,** and **corn oil,** for example, have bland flavors that impart no distinctive character of their own and may be heated without burning to the high temperatures necessary for frying. **Olive oil,** by contrast, has a distinctive taste and aroma derived from the fruit of the olive tree. It is favored in the Mediterranean kitchen. Extra-virgin olive oil, the highest grade, is extracted on the first pressing without use of heat or chemicals, making it the oil of choice for dressings and marinades, while filtered pure olive oil has less character but may be heated to higher temperatures for general cooking.

ONIONS

The pungent flavor of all kinds of onions enhances chicken dishes. **Green onions** (below), also called spring onions or scallions, are a variety harvested immature, leaves and all, before their bulbs have formed. Both their green tops and white bulbs are appreciated for their mild but still pronounced onion flavor. **Red (Spanish) onions** are a mild, sweet variety with purplish red skin and red-tinged white flesh. **Yellow onions,** the most common variety, have white flesh and a strong flavor; they are easily recognized by their dry, yellowish brown skins.

SHALLOTS

These members of the onion family have paper-thin brown skin that encloses pale, purple-tinged flesh. The mild flavor of shallots is appreciated in a wide variety of chicken dishes.

SPICES

A wide range of spices enlivens chicken dishes. It is best to buy any kind of spice in small quantities from a store that has a regular turnover of inventory, as flavors tend to diminish rapidly. Store spices in airtight containers away from heat and light.

CAYENNE PEPPER

Finely ground from the dried cayenne chile, this powdered seasoning is spicy hot in flavor and orange-red or orange in color.

CUMIN SEEDS

Small, crescent-shaped seeds used in Middle Eastern, Indian, and Mexican kitchens, this spice adds a strong, dusky flavor and aroma.

CURRY POWDER

The term *curry powder* describes complex Indian blends of spices usually including coriander, cumin, ground dried chile, fenugreek, and turmeric, as well as cardamom, cinnamon, cloves, allspice, fennel seeds, and ginger.

PAPRIKA

This powdered spice is made from the dried paprika pepper, available in sweet, mild, and hot forms. Hungarian paprika is considered the best quality, but milder Spanish paprika may also be used.

SAFFRON

Perhaps the rarest of spices, saffron is derived from the dried stigmas of a species of crocus, sold either as threads or powdered. It gives intensely aromatic flavor and bright golden orange color to classic Mediterranean and Indian dishes.

TOMATOES

A popular complement to chicken, tomatoes add their sweet flavor and robust texture to a variety of recipes, including slow-cooked stews and pasta dishes featuring chicken, and to barbecue sauces for grilled chicken. When ripened on the vine beneath the summer sun, tomatoes approach perfection. If sun-ripened tomatoes are not available, the most reliable choice for good tomato flavor and texture at any time of year is the **plum (Roma)** (below)

tomato. In many recipes, canned plum tomatoes may also be substituted, whether whole or crushed; some recipes may call for puréed and seasoned canned tomatoes or concentrated tomato paste to bolster the flavor. In all cases, seek out the best brand available.

To peel a fresh tomato, using a small, sharp knife, cut out its core, immerse in boiling water for about 20 seconds, and then transfer to a bowl of ice water. The skin should peel off easily, either with your fingertips or with the assistance of the knife. To seed the tomato, cut it in half horizontally and gently squeeze each half to force out the seed sacs.

ZEST

The outermost, brightly colored layer of a citrus fruit's rind is rich in essential oils that flavor savory and sweet dishes alike. Citrus zest may be removed in various ways: in small particles with a fine grater; in thin strips with a swivel-bladed vegetable peeler or a special citrus "stripper"; or in fine shreds with the small, sharp-edged holes of a citrus "zester." In every case, care should be taken not to remove any of the thick layer of bitter white pith beneath the zest.

INDEX

ACKNOWLEDGMENTS

The publishers would like to thank the following people and associations for their generous assistance and support in producing this book: Desne Border, Ken DellaPenta, Jennifer Hanson, Hill Nutrition Associates, Lisa Lee, and Cecily Upton.

The following kindly lent props for photography: Fillamento, San Francisco, CA; Williams-Sonoma and Pottery Barn, San Francisco, CA. The photographer would like to thank Pavlina Eccless for generously sharing her home with us for our location setting. We would also like to thank Chromeworks and ProCamera, San Francisco, CA, and FUJI Film for their generous support of this project. Special acknowledgment goes to Daniel Yearwood for the beautiful backgrounds and surface treatments.